CREATED FOR A PURPOSE

By
Gladys Oni

Unveiling the Truth of How Useful You Are
in God's World of Making Things Happen

CREATED FOR A PURPOSE
Copyright © 2011 Gladys Oni

ISBN: 978-1-907011-24-5

Published in the United Kingdom by:
EsteemWorld Publications

British Library Cataloguing In Publication Data
A Record of this Publication is available from the British Library.

Printed in Great Britain for EsteemWorld Publications

DEDICATION

This book is dedicated to God the father, Son and Holy Ghost who put it in my heart to write it even when I did not know that I had the gift to write. To you be all the glory my Lord and king.

ACKNOWLEDGMENTS

I would like to express my profound gratitude to my darling daughters Faith and Sandra whose love, support and understanding, helped me in the completion of this book.

I would also like to thank pastor Jojo Mercy Bialugaba for proof reading and contributions made and I am grateful to pastor Bert Phagan for his support.

My profound gratitude also goes to Denise Felton who edited this book.

My greatest thanks goes to our God who is the author of all creation

Table of Contents

Introduction

Why was I created? What is my purpose? These are questions that would capture our thoughts as we look at the title of this book.

Today, if you are holding this book in your hands, know that it is not by accident. You may have been searching and longing to know your purpose or why you were created. Or you may want to help someone discover their purpose. So take your time to read and allow the Holy Spirit to help you understand the entire message of the book. You can know the truth concerning your purpose here on earth. The Bible tells us in John 8:32 "And you shall know the truth, and the truth shall make you free."

Since Creation, the sun and the moon have been functioning very well, and have blessed mankind. When it is time for the sun to rise, it begins to shine. That is called "day." When it is time for the sun to set and go down, it does so. Darkness sets in and this is known as "night." It is known as the major source of light and heat to the world. The moon also knows its time and season to shine and glow – showing off its beauty, and it gives light and joy to all the world. Both the sun and moon have faithfully been doing their jobs ever since they were made, thus fulfilling the purpose of why they were created. We cannot imagine a world without the sun and the moon, because they help us in calculating dates and events. As we know the purposes of the sun and moon, so you ought to know your place and your purpose in destiny.

Find out the purpose why you were created and begin to regularly function by being a blessing to your world and generation. Just know that you were created for a purpose, destined to shine, and born to win.

CHAPTER 1 - The God of Authority:

The Creator Transferred Authority to Us to CREATE Like Himself

Genesis 1:1, 2a, 3 say:

> *"In the beginning God created the heavens and the earth. 2 The earth was without form, and void; and darkness was on the face of the deep. Then God said, "Let there be light"; and there was light."*

As you read further in the chapter referenced above, you will find that God began speaking everything into existence, and then in verse 26, He says "Let us [God the Father, God the Son and God the Holy Spirit] make man in our image, after our likeness: and let them have dominion over the fish of the sea, and over the fowl of the air, and over the cattle, and over all the earth, and over every creeping thing that creepeth upon the earth."

This is how highly esteemed of God you are – that He would bestow His authority on you. Do not shy away from using this power and the great privilege that He conferred on you when you were born again. God made man in His own image and likeness so that we could also create just as God Himself can. He made you to have dominion over everything, including all trials during your time on earth. So, my beloved, walk in this truth, knowing that you were made more than a conqueror. Do not allow your situation to overcome you.

In Genesis chapter 3, where Adam and Eve sinned, the authority that God had given to Man was lost – or given away. The First Adam turned and gave his authority to the serpent – Satan. But Jesus came to the earth expressed, so that He would die on the Cross to redeem us from sin. Second Corinthians 5:21 says: "For He made Him who knew no sin to be sin for us, that we might become the righteousness of God in Him."

But when He arose, the God-given authority was restored to Man. And, to as many as received Jesus as Lord and believed on His name, He gave power to become the sons of God (John 1:12). This means that the name of Jesus belongs to you and you need to use the authority that's in that name to defeat the devil and all his works. Use it to locate and fulfil your purpose here on earth. God gave you authority so you could win; therefore, do not remain passive, but be confident to use it by taking your position, and things will work right for you.

Here is what it says in Ephesians 6:10:

> *"Finally, my brethren, be strong in the Lord and in the power of His might."*

It is encouraging to know that you are the one that God gave power and authority to. Until you realize this, you cannot exercise your rights. So, do not be afraid of the devil or tremble before him anymore. Be strong. No matter the situation before you right now, be confident and know that you have the power to do all things in the name of Jesus, and only in His name. There is one thing that you must know, and that is, for you to have authority, you must submit to authority – the highest authority, being God Himself. The Creator sees what you are doing with the power that He has given to you, so you must use it. You must not become passive, nor must you abuse this power. You have authority over every power other than the One that appointed you. And the authority of our God is the highest. He has the final say over all creatures, and the best part of it is that He is on your side.

Many years ago, I attended a mixed secondary school as a boarder staying in the dormitory with other students. I was appointed as the female house prefect of the red house. (Note: A prefect, generally, is a student who is given some authority over other pupils in matters of discipline in a private school.) I remember that I was very small and quiet, and there were older girls in my house who were bigger than I and were stubborn.

The school knew that I could lead well in that position, hence my appointment. And although it came to me as a surprise, I accepted it with great confidence. The house master in charge of my house was the vice principal of the school I was submitting to, and he was a man the students feared a lot. In the course of leading, sometimes some of the stubborn girls would break the rules and refuse the punishments I gave to them. I refused to be afraid of them and went to report such cases to my housemaster. He in turn stepped in to rectify things, and they eventually had no choice but to obey the small and quiet me. I was very young and was not a born-again Christian then, but I knew and understood the authority I had. There were things I had to quit doing, or else the students would have taken me for granted and I would have been seen as breaking the rules.

There was an incident in which my house ranked last in the random inspection of the dormitories by the school inspectors because one of the girls did not tidy up her bed properly. My house master was angry with me and felt that I failed to supervise properly that day. He kept me in detention for hours. As a result of this, I was very angry and told him that I did not want to be a prefect anymore. But later we talked things over and apologized to one another. He encouraged me to remain, but said that I must strive to do better. I strove hard and tried not to be last again, and there were those times we came out first. I was glad I had not quit because I gained a lot of experience. I had great confidence and a positive attitude in dealing with issues that came my way. In the face of rebuke, when I had given up on and wanted someone else to take my place, as a good overseer, the house master knew that I had what it took to lead the girls in that house, and he encouraged me to not give up.

In the same way you ought to recognize that your authority is from God – the highest power. He has put everything in place to make you succeed in life. Just as my house master was there for me at all times to help me, even more is God always on the scene to help you. So, do not discard the authority you have to create blessings all around you. Do not discount the power you have been given to live the dream that God wants you to have. You may have given up on everything and lack the will to fight to achieve your dreams. Go to the Word of God and be encouraged. Take back your authority and fight until you fulfil your purpose. Do not die and don't allow your dreams to die. In the face of difficulty, let God guide you like my house master guided me through God's Word. Let God teach you how to use the power and authority He has given to you so you can rule your circumstances with ease and come out triumphantly.

In John 14:12, Jesus said:

> *"Most assuredly, I say to you, he who believes in Me, the works that I do he will do also; and greater works than these he will do, because I go to My Father."*

Great works are in you, so speak them forth. Create manifold miracles. As much as possible, believe in yourself and be confident and bold enough to stand on the authority of God's Word. Remember that we are joint heirs with Christ Jesus (Romans 8:17). God quickened the dead and called those things that be not as though they were. He spoke the worlds and everything in them into existence, (Romans 4:17-19). The New King James version says it this way:

> *"God...gives life to the dead and calls those things which do not exist as though they did."*

That is how we are supposed to speak forth our heart's desires. The world was without form and void and God began to create. So you ought to create life and speak life into every void in your vision or situation. You have been equipped to succeed, so do not give up. Hold on to God's Word until life is brought back into that situation.

Imagine that you were representing your country in a relay and each athlete would hand over their baton to the next person. When it was your turn, instead of keeping up with the pace to play your part, you dropped the baton and walked away, sobbing out of fear of losing and lack of motivation to carry on. The end result is that you would have disappointed your country and the spectators. Above all, you would have been a big failure to yourself because you threw away the chance to bring victory to your country. Afterwards, your coach comes to counsel you and he encourages you not to give up next time, but to run the race to the end with the thought of winning. When the next season came, you went out there with so much confidence and you won the race. You played your part well and you made yourself and everyone proud. Just as people were watching and waiting to see if you were going to stop halfway again, so your generation is waiting for you to play your part to bless them.

Today, it may be that the pressures of life have confused you and put fear in you. Perhaps you have become complacent with failure and sitting on the fence of life. I am encouraging and exhorting you to rediscover the authority in the Word of God. You can move mightily in every area of your life to affect your generation. God is faithful and just, and He will surely see you through, so make use of the authority that He has given to you.

Wake up from your sleep. Pray and cast out the spirit of fear (timidity) from your life. Do not slumber, do not complain, and do not fear. Take authority over the situation and create life and miracles the way God does. Take charge of your own mind. Take charge of your own destiny. That is not God's job, it's your job. Do not allow thoughts of failure. Your mind is the battlefield between God and the devil, so do not allow it to become a dustbin for sinful thoughts. As much as possible, control your thoughts and renew your mind with the Word of God. Sing songs of praise to the Lord and worship Him.

1 Peter 3:22 says:

> *"[Christ] has gone into heaven and is at the right hand of God, [and] angels and authorities and powers [have] been made subject to Him."*

This same authority over all power has been given to us and conferred on us. Once you begin to realize this, you will take control over territorial demons and familiar spirits that are causing all manner of problems in your life. You have the authority to nullify the handwriting against you. Stand firm and take control over every power that is against your family, your finance, and your dreams.

Philippians 2:10-11 says:

> *" [At] the name of Jesus every knee should bow, of those in heaven, and of those on earth, and of those under the earth, and that every tongue should confess that Jesus Christ is Lord, to the glory of God the Father."*

All knees bow at the mention of the name of Jesus and at the professing of the power in His blood. We have been given power over all manner of spirits, as it says in Matthew 10:1:

> *"And when He had called His twelve disciples to Him, He gave them power over unclean spirits, to cast them out, and to heal all kinds of sickness and all kinds of disease."*

The disciples did not have the authority to heal the sick and cast out devils until Jesus gave it to them. Then they began to go in that power, once they did, signs and wonders followed them. In the same way, you have been called out and given power and authority to do exploits in the name of Jesus.

In Mark 4:35-41, Jesus told His disciples that they were going to cross over to the other side of the Sea of Galilee, where they had been. They entered the ship and other small ships followed. Then, a great windstorm began to beat waves against the ship. Jesus was asleep in the rear of the ship. The disciples woke Him up asking if He cared that they could perish. Jesus simply took authority over the storm and said to the sea "Peace, be still!" Suddenly, there was great calm. He later rebuked the disciples for being afraid and for not having any faith. When they eventually got to the other side, He healed a man with an unclean spirit, whom no one could help or hold down, not even with chains.

This is how we out to be – just like Jesus. You can have peace when you are facing the storms of life. But you must make use of your authority, by your confession of faith in God's word. The anointing for your breakthrough is in you. Just as the man was tormented for many years until Jesus set him free, so are the lives of many who are bound and waiting for you to set them free. Many people are waiting for you to give them hope to live again. You cannot afford to remain in the storms of life and do nothing about them. If you continue to do nothing, you will die with unfulfilled dreams. You cannot remain in a rut. Take a step of faith to change your situation. Use the authority you have. Many lives are waiting to receive their deliverance through you.

Just as Jesus kept doing something good for God, that is what God expects of you. There is no time to waste. You have been given the same power that Jesus had. And though Satan may rage by bringing fierce trials your way, you can be confident that you will never be defeated because you have the power to be victorious in the war, because Jesus already won the battle for you. A man of authority stands up straight and tall. He is full of confidence and knows the source of his strength.

I have never seen a law enforcement agent, such as the police or the military, acting lifeless when they have to stop someone to create order. They are well-armed, and have the power and the authority to use force against any lawbreaker. In the same way, you are a soldier in the army of the Lord. You do not have to cry or beg. Because you have on the whole armor of God, you have the authority to create order where there is disorder in your life and environment. You have the power to chase away all demonic activities. Do not shy away from using the mandate that has been given to you. Change, transform, restore and resurrect everything around you that the enemy has stolen, spoiled, or destroyed.

Like me, I would encourage you to resolve that you will never leave what belongs to you in the hands of the enemy. With God on your side, you are well able to claim all that belongs to you and to live a purposeful life.

CHAPTER 2 - Born for a Purpose
You Are a Special Person. You Are Not Useless.

God knew each of us before we were born. In fact, He told Jeremiah that He knew him before He (God Himself) formed Jeremiah in the womb of his mother. God said that even then – before Jeremiah was born – God ordained that he would be a prophet to the nations.

And not only Jeremiah, but He specially made man – every man – for a purpose here on earth, and it was first of all, to worship Him. Pause and think of this. Logically and biologically speaking, the male sperm fertilizes the female ovary before reproduction takes place. And out of over one million sperm, only the one that could form you won the race. A very short time afterwards, the other spermatozoa died. As a matter of fact, at this stage before your parents met, God had already known your correct form, how you would look, your name, your carrier and everything about you. The DNA that is unique to you was God's idea.

This means that it was also within His power not to have formed you at all. But He made it possible for you to be born into this world...for a divine purpose.

Scripture says in Ecclesiastes 3:1-8:

> *"To every thing there is a season, and a time to every purpose under the heaven: A time to be born, and a time to die; a time to plant, and a time to pluck up that which is planted; A time to kill, and a time to heal; a time to break down, and a time to build up; A time to weep, and a time to laugh; a time to mourn, and a time to dance; A time to cast away stones, and a time to gather stones together; a time to embrace and a time to refrain from embracing; A time to get, and a time to lose; a time to keep, and a time to cast away; A time to rend, and a time to sew; a time to keep silence, and a time to speak; A time to love and a time to hate; a time of war and a time of peace."*

Every person needs to find out what there is for him or her to accomplish on the earth. First and foremost, we were created to serve God and to live for Him alone. After that, we must make use of the many talents that He deposited in us to fulfil our destiny and the destiny of others. You are not a mistake, even if your parents say you were conceived by mistake. The truth is, God formed you and knew you were going to be born, and He loaded you with great abilities that are to be discovered and used. So you need to take time to find out the purpose that you were born.

We should try to find out the right profession God wants for us, and the right area where we should serve in the church. It is important that we know the calling of God in our lives. It is sad to know that some people go through life doing whatever comes their way, without ever knowing their purpose here on the earth. Pursue that purpose with passion and vigor, and enthusiasm. Arise and shine, because you are a very special light.

Some years ago, as I was going through 1 Peter, I received a revelation that I am a princess, royalty of the heavenly kingdom:

> *"But ye are a chosen generation, a royal priesthood, an holy nation, a peculiar people; that ye should show forth the praises of Him who hath called you out of darkness into His marvellous light" (v. 2:9)*

Since then, my attitude towards life changed in terms of the way I see myself and carry myself – in spite of the difficult times I've had. I became so confident in God and in myself that I refused to allow the pressures of life to keep me from fulfilling my calling.

And likewise, there is royalty in you. There is a king or a queen on the inside of you that the world needs to see, and only you can show forth the power and ability to reign over all of your circumstances.

God made us all equal but different, each of us with many different gifts and abilities within us to help attain our goals. Some people have songs inside them that have never been heard or sung. They have books and poems inside them that have never been published, plays and arts that have never been exhibited. There are businesses that have not been established. Various dreams have gone unfulfilled. Now is a good time to accomplish those dreams.

Don't try to be anyone else, because you have a unique and special gift to bless your world. Decide to be not just who you are, but who you were meant to be. You are special. You are one of a kind. You are a wonderful and marvellous creation. In Psalm 139:14, David says *"I will praise You, for I am fearfully and wonderfully made; marvellous are Your works, and that my soul knows very well."*

In the Bible, Gideon and the Israelites were oppressed for many years by the Midianites because they had sinned against God. Finally, they cried out to Him for help and He had mercy on them. He sent an angel to Gideon where he was busy threshing wheat by the winepress – in hiding because he feared the Midianites. The angel told him that God was going to use him to deliver his people out of bondage. The angel called him a "mighty man of valor," but Gideon looked down on himself and did not think that he could help his people. He began to give different excuses why he could not do what God wanted him to do. At last, he began to believe in himself and see himself in the way that God saw him – as a mighty man of valor – as a courageous man. Gideon went on to deliver the Midianites, just as God had earlier said (Judges 6:1-14).

This may be the position you are in right now. Having lost confidence in yourself, you are in hiding and do not want anyone to get too close to you. You don't want anyone to find out some things about you – things that have been eating you up. Things you are not proud of. Things that no one knows about. Even when God is assuring you through His Word or through men of God that you can come out of that situation, you still look down on yourself and prefer to remain in that position where you are – the position of defeat.

Right now you may not have food on your table, clothes in your closet, or a roof over your head. You may not have money to pay bills, and you may be pressed on every side by every unimaginable problem. You may be divorced, widowed, a single parent, uneducated, or not eloquent in speech. You might have a chronic disease or be in a different difficult situation. But as you read this book, I decree that you are going to believe the report of the Lord concerning you: Jeremiah 32 : 29 says:

> *"Behold, I am the LORD, the God of all flesh. Is there anything too hard for Me?"*

In Luke 1, it says:

> *"For with God nothing shall be impossible" (v.37).*

The Bible makes us to know that every person has a purpose here on earth – every person...in our families, our churches, in our society and the world. Look inside yourself prayerfully. Find out the reason why you were created. Do not give up because of various discouraging circumstances that surround you. If you will look carefully, it will amaze you to know that many people are fulfilling their dreams in spite of all the odds against them. You can do the same. You can be on the winning team. Jesus Christ, whose footsteps we follow, fulfilled His purpose by setting the captives free, loosing those who were bound, healing the sick, and raising up the dead. And finally, He died for the sins of the world and brought salvation to us all. He passed through difficult and trying times along the way, but He was not distracted. His purpose was not overshadowed by alternative choices that would have been second-hand at best. He stuck to His original vision and lived a fulfilled life.

It is time for us to start living a victorious life of accomplishments.

I never thought or imagined that one day I would be able to write a book. I did not know that I had the talent or the gift to write. And then one day I discovered this talent and I worked toward it. Today, you are being blessed by it.

As a matter of fact, I started writing this book in 1991 when I was still in my home country of Nigeria. I kept on working on it, but I could not complete and publish it due to different factors. In 2002, when I arrived in Belgium, I was further discouraged and could not do much about it because of the language barrier, as Belgium is predominantly a French- and Dutch-speaking country.

Finally, a door opened for me to move to England in 2007, and it was by the grace of God that I knew it was time to publish it. I had to tidy up my work and put all efforts in to publish. It was not that simple to do, but God helped me as I took that step of faith. Well, today, you are reading that which God had said would come to be –20 years ago.

I thank God that one of the reasons why God made me was to write this book – and that has been fulfilled. Some people were called by God into the five-fold ministry – that is, to be an apostle, or a prophet, or an evangelist, or a pastor or teacher. The scripture says that He called people to fill those positions so that the saints of God would be perfected. He called them to the work of the ministry, or for the building of it. And that ministry continues for the edifying of the Body of Christ (Ephesians 4:11- 12).

Has God appointed you to fill one of those positions? Has he anointed you to fill one of them? Make sure you are doing what God wants you to do. If you feel that you were called to be an evangelist, then go ahead and preach, for if you do not, you will have missed your purpose in life. Discover it – or rediscover it before it is too late. In John 9:4, Jesus says:

> *"I must work the works of Him who sent Me while it is day; the night is coming when no one can work."*

Here, Jesus is simply saying not to procrastinate. He is saying that if you do, there will surely come a time when you will not be able to do what you were called to do. In the common vernacular, it could be translated to mean "Strike while the iron is hot" or "Make hay while the sun shines."

It is time to stop sitting down on your problems and stand up for Jesus – fast! Stop making excuses. Begin to plan positive strategies to move on with the creative and inventive part of your life. It is pathetic each time someone goes to the grave with unfulfilled dreams and aspirations, and with an unfulfilled life. The only difference between those who achieve their goals in life and those who don't is a simple step of faith. That is it! So, take action now concerning your vision. Every day, do something about it and all will surely be well in God's time. Do not be afraid that you will fail if you try. You are a failure only if you don't try at all. If it does not go the way you believe it should, try again. Quit blaming others and keep praying, and you will eventually make it. Have faith in God and in yourself. Come out of your shell. Be courageous, be confident. Identify what your passions are and invest all you are and all you have in that direction. Stay focused, be diligent and hold on.

Sometime ago, there was a visiting preacher from England at Praise Centre, which was my church in Brussels, Belgium. This preacher said that he had been doing fine as a young businessman, but went on to be the first person to become a Christian in his family. When God called him to be an evangelist, he kept working at his business. But he was not happy until he made the decision that changed his life for good. He obeyed God and went into full-time ministry. God eventually blessed him with a wife and son, and has been with him all the way, so he has never regretted that decision.

He was glad that he found his purpose. I pray that you will also find yours and allow it to come to pass through Jesus Christ our Lord. Amen!

CHAPTER 3 - Sanctified for a Purpose
Remain Sanctified

Right from our mother's womb, the Lord God Almighty sanctified us and set us apart from all manner of evil.

In Jeremiah 1:5, it says:

> *"Before I formed thee in the belly I knew thee; and before thou came forth out of the womb I sanctified thee, and I ordained thee a prophet unto the nations."*

Here, to be "sanctified" simply means that Jeremiah was specially cleansed and set apart for a divine purpose by God right from the womb. We have also been sanctified, and we ought to remain in that purified state continuously.

Jesus himself also prayed to God the father to sanctify us as in John 17:17-19, which says:

> *"Sanctify them through thy truth: thy word is truth. As thou hast sent me into the world, even so have I also*

sent them into the world. And for
their sakes I sanctify myself, that
they also might be sanctified through
the truth."

Let us learn to live in the truth of the Word of God, as only then we can be cleansed to fulfil destiny. John 15:3 says:

"Now ye are clean through the word
which I have spoken unto you."

There is no alternative to living the Bible way or living a Godly life. God set us apart here on earth for that purpose – right from the womb, so we have to follow His Word to achieve a purposeful life. Examine yourself to see if you are living every day according to the Word of God.

After tasting of heavenly things and declaring that we are for Jesus, you are to remain purified so that God's purpose might be accomplished in your life. The reason why some of us have problems with our life seeming purposeless is because we live carelessly and recklessly. We forget the Rock from which we were hewed. We should sanctify our lives on a daily basis. We need the Word of God daily to see us along our various paths. Christianity is a way of life. It is not a habit to pick up or a hobby to practice. It should become our nature and become effortless – like inhaling and exhaling.

Romans 12:1-2 says:

> *"I beseech you therefore, brethren, by the mercies of God, that ye present your bodies a living sacrifice, holy, acceptable unto God, which is your reasonable service. And be not conformed to this world: but be ye transformed by the renewing of your mind, that ye may prove what is that good, and acceptable, and perfect, will of God."*

It should not be distressing or upsetting to live a sanctified life. The Apostle Paul says that a life of sacrifice is not too much to ask of us. It is not too much for God to ask that we live pleasing to Him. Let the Word of God change your negative mindset into a more optimistic way of thinking and a more positive way of doing things in line with the Word of God.

God specially prepared Mary, the mother of our Lord Jesus Christ mentally, physically and spiritually. And He prepared her womb for our

Saviour, and sanctified Him in it as the seed that would go on to do great works. In that same way, God made your mother's womb to house you and set you apart until you were born. Jesus had been set apart, but when He realized that He was called, He worked with God to bring it to pass. He cooperated with His Father and went on to perform miracles and wonders. If you realize that the same ability is available to you as you walk in truth, you will be sure to fulfil your destiny.

Romans 8:11 says: "If the Spirit of Him who raised Jesus from the dead dwells in you, He who raised Christ from the dead will also give life to your mortal bodies." God will quicken you. He will give you life. He will cause you to become alive!!!

2 Corinthians 6:14-18 says:

> *"Be ye not unequally yoked together with unbelievers: for what fellowship hath righteousness with unrighteousness? And what communion hath light with darkness? And what concord hath Christ with Belial? or what part hath he that believeth with an infidel? And what agreement hath the temple of God with idols? For ye are the temple*

of the living God; as Goth hath said, I will dwell in them, and walk in them; and I will be their God, and they shall be my people. Wherefore come out from among them, and be ye separate, saith the Lord, and touch not the unclean thing; and I will receive you, And will be a Father unto you, and ye shall be my sons and daughters, saith the Lord Almighty."

When light is shined in a dark room, it lights the place. The room becomes bright and people can see clearly. So our lives ought to be. We know the scripture says that we live in the world but we are not of the world (see John 15:19). So wherever we find ourselves in the midst of people who do evil works, we are not supposed to be corrupted by them, but we are to maintain our identity as God-fearing people, separated and sanctified – or set apart – unto good works. Our bodies make up the temple of the Holy Ghost, so we cannot live like people who do not know Him. In an ungodly society and environment like ours today, we should do away with the slogan that says "If you can't beat them, join them."

In 1992, I remember walking along the streets of Nigeria, going to work on the night shift as a nurse. The Lord dropped a song in my heart and I quickly wrote it down. The song was a warning to me so I would not fall into temptation that lay ahead of me. I sang the song all the way through. The temptation came and, thank God, I did not yield, because the Lord had warned me ahead of time. I have been singing that song ever since. It is a reminder of the price that Jesus paid for us on the Cross of Calvary. The song goes like this:

> "Be wise, is the counsel of God
> Be wise, is the counsel of God
> Do not act foolishly,
> For you were bought with a price
> Be wise, be wise in the Lord."

Galatians 5:1 says:

> *"Stand fast therefore in the liberty by which Christ has made us free, and do not be entangled again with a yoke of bondage."*

It is difficult to know or accomplish one's dream and purpose in life when you go forward and backward, backsliding from the presence of God. An unstable person cannot know the purpose of his existence for James 1:8 says:

"A double minded man is unstable in all his ways."

When a dog returns to its vomit, it is disgusting and repulsive! That is how it is with people who after knowing Jesus, return to their sin. We have been sanctified by God, so let us remain that way. Only when we purge ourselves from all manner of sin can God make use of us. Only then can we clearly achieve our goals.

CHAPTER 4 - Ordained to Create
Faith in Action

God has ordained you unto good works from before the foundations of the earth. Whether you are young or old, you need to realize that just as He called Jeremiah to be a prophet, so He has called you to do that which He has placed before you.

God has ordained you for a divine purpose and He wants you to take a bold step of faith. Act on His Word, because He has predestined you for it. Jesus declared in Luke 4:18-19

> *"The Spirit of the LORD is upon Me, because He has anointed Me to preach the gospel to the poor; He has sent Me to heal the brokenhearted to proclaim liberty to the captives and recovery of sight to the blind, to set at liberty those who are oppressed; to proclaim the acceptable year of the LORD."*

Your miracle is in your hands, and you were created to bring that vision to pass. Act fast and move in God's timing, which is right now. Exercise your faith now. Hebrews 11:1-3 says:

> *"Now faith is the substance of things hoped for, the evidence of things not seen. For by it the elders obtained a good testimony. By faith we understand that the worlds were framed by the word of God, so that the things which are seen were not made of things which are visible."*

It is only by faith that miracles can be created through the spoken Word of God. Use your divinely ordained power to create and invent new things by speaking out loud the Word of God. You are on a mission here on earth, so search the Scriptures and ask God, so you can know where you fit in – that is, so you can know what your calling is, and so that you can be about your Father's business.

Change your attitude, your language, and all the negative things around you. Begin to see things positively as you start declaring the Word of God over your life until you are able to tap into that creative power.

Hebrews 11:6 says:

> *"But without faith it is impossible to please Him, for he who comes to God must believe that He is, and that He is a rewarder of those who diligently seek Him."*

Learn to fix your heart on winning at all times, for the winner's crown was placed on you since before the foundations of the world. Start declaring that you can make it and see yourself through Christ who strengthens you (Philippians 4:13). The anointing of God is upon you to enable you to do what the Lord has assigned you to here on earth. The anointing of God on your life must be used, for you were not anointed to only feel good and enjoy God's presence. You must use that anointing to change your situation and the situations of others who don't know Christ as you do.

I challenge you right now confront adverse situations. Call destiny forward in your life. Walk with a level of faith that you have never exercised before. Faithfully give your offerings. Tithe more than ever before. Faithfully attend worship services like you have never done. Love and forgive as never before. Use your gifts as never before. Fast and pray as you have never done.

Evangelize because people are dying every day without knowing God. Many have not heard the Gospel of Jesus Christ as you could share it with them. Sing songs of praise and worship God as you have never done, and above all, learn to be silent in His presence more than before so that He could speak back to you. 1 John 2:20 says

> *"But you have an anointing (an unction [KJV] from the Holy One, and you know all things."*

The Word of God encourages us to put on the whole armour of God and to take the shield of faith to quench the fiery darts of the wicked one (Ephesians 6:13-17). This may find you in "I cannot make it" frustrations, doubts and problem situations of all kinds, but if you are able to renew your mind with the Word of God, then you will certainly win.

Learn to have faith in your faith. That was how Abraham (formerly called Abram) and his wife Sarah (formerly known as Sarai), had faith in God and were called by their miracle names long before the promised child Isaac was born (as told in Genesis 17:1-14). Faith in action, or active faith, is when you confess your vision, believe it, and work towards that goal. You see yourself as a winner before you see it come to pass in the physical. As a matter of fact, whatever takes place in the physical realm has already been in the spiritual realm. And we need eyes of faith to see it, the heart of faith to desire it, the mouth of faith to speak forth our miracles, and the power of faith to believe and pull down our goals into the physical realm. Jesus is our perfect example, and if we must succeed, we have to look to Him for help, because He is the author and finisher of our faith (Hebrews 12:2).

Some years ago in a conference, a woman testified of how she had been healed of barrenness as she went to touch the hem of the garment of a great man of God of the Church of God Mission International, Inc. It was the late Archbishop Benson Idahosa. After many years of not being able to bear children, this woman conceived, and she came with the testimony child. In fact, there were many of this kind of testimony in this ministry, which happened to be my church in Nigeria back then.

Also, in one of our women's conferences in Nigeria, when a woman of God was preaching, she asked all those who were barren to go and make urine immediately whether they felt like it or not. She said that they would become pregnant. Many believed in the prophetic word that came and did so. Months later, some became pregnant and had babies; one of them was from my particular branch of this local church.

When we act in faith on God's Word spoken into our lives through Men or Women of God or when we act in faith by ourselves directly on His word, circumstances change instantaneously. We may have believed God for answers to some issues in our lives for many years. We may have prayed and done all we knew how to do. But one word from the Lord or one prophetic action from Him through anyone can change the situation in just a twinkle of an eye.

There is power in positive thinking and speaking. Believe the Word of God and prophesy over life, for you have power and can move mountains out of your way by faith (Matthew 17:19-20).

> *"The disciples came to Jesus privately and said, "Why could we not cast it out?" So Jesus said to them, "Because of your unbelief; for assuredly, I say to you, if you have faith as a mustard*

seed, you will say to this mountain, 'Move from here to there,' and it will move; and nothing will be impossible for you."

The mark of an achiever is to be able to continuously pray God's kingdom into and over his own life (and that of others) and into all situations around him here on earth. He confesses that the will of God for his or her own life will be done just as it is in heaven. You need to start asking questions from people who you know who have experience in that area of your goal. Start reading books and listening to messages that point in the direction of your goal. The fact is that you must do something that prepares you towards your dream after you have identified what they are. Where there has been joblessness, you should prayerfully send out applications to different offices again and again even if they keep turning you down and one day, a positive reply from one of them will surely come at God's time.

When you're troubled about your vision or the call of God on you, release the Word of God concerning it. The Word is spirit and life, so send it forth to hover all around it. Faith believes something strongly and holds tenaciously to that belief. It does not let go, for faith says it must surely come to pass.

In a football pitch, towards the end of the match, there is the injury time when pressure from both teams is fiercest. Most times, the strongest team that exacts the most pressure scores the goal. At the last minute, a goal may be scored where it had seemed impossible for almost an hour of playing time and of hard work chasing the ball around the field. What happened? It shows that you should never say the game is over until it really is -- when the referee has blown the final whistle. So it is with our Christian race and aspirations. So long as you have the breath of life, keep on pushing and pursue your goal with all you have got, until you give birth to it.

Isaiah 10:27 says:

> *"And it shall come to pass in that day, that his burden shall be taken away from off thy shoulder, and his yoke from off thy neck, and the yoke shall be destroyed because of the anointing."*

Since God ordained you as a believer, His anointing in you is meant to break every yoke of bondage. Spend quality time each day to review different strategies and plans made available to you to make your dream come true. Write down possibilities, ask questions, and as you do, strike out some things and add new ones. Begin to act on each step and something will surely happen. A business idea may come to you. Prayerfully do a feasibility study on your idea or dream, and see what God will do with the step of faith that you take.

The woman with the issue of blood for twelve years knew no physician who could help (Matthew 9), but she had great faith that Jesus would heal her. With her unquenchable faith, she pressed through the crowd, telling herself that if only she could touch the hem of Jesus' garment, she would become whole. As unbelievable as it might have seemed to anyone else, it happened just as she thought it would. Maybe that is why Scripture records that she "said within herself ...". She probably did not expect anyone to believe that she could be healed of a condition that she had for twelve years.

This woman fought against a weak body, pain, self-pity, lack of finances, and more that we will never know. Bleeding for twelve years would leave anyone weak, so how was she able to press through the crowd? She didn't dwell on all the obstacles, she just took a step of faith – a leap of faith – and she was healed. Because she was determined, her faith gave her the ability. Notice that in Matthew 9:22, Jesus said to her, "Thy faith hath made thee whole.

Your faith can make you whole. It can enable you to accomplish, attain, and achieve anything you believe that God wants for you, or anything He wants you to do.

I was officially ordained as a deaconess some years ago in my church in Nigeria. I had been functioning as an adult Sunday School/Bible teacher and as a women's leader of one of the four groups in my local church. I trusted God to do my job very well. I knew I was ordained and had to be conscious of that fact at all times to live up to expectations. My time, money and the whole of me went into serving well in that office with the anointing that came with it. I attended seminars and conferences with others and learned how to serve the people better. I had to follow up and visit the people I was serving and pray for them. I did all I could for them, but trusted God to help me, otherwise I would not have been able to do it. Even Jesus, who is God, knew that He was ordained to save lives and to help people, and He had faith in God and did all kinds of miracles.

When Lazarus died and was buried, Jesus called him forth to life. He told the people to remove the grave clothes that had bound him, to turn him loose and allow him to go free, and it was so. Jesus was ordained to create miracles. He had faith in God and knew that when He prayed, God heard Him – always. (See John 11:33– 44.) In the same manner you have been ordained officially by God and you have the anointing in you to help you fulfil your purpose. Search the Scriptures, attend Bible studies and conferences, read Bible-teaching books. Do something with all you have learned and as you act on the Word of God by faith, you will surely succeed.

Whether your problem is marital, physical, spiritual – whatever – there are Bible verses to address them all. You can anchor your faith to change these ugly situations. The faith signal says "no stopping, get going." Move into the realm of faith and refuse to give up. Victory will surely come your way.

CHAPTER 5 - Faith Sayings

1. The just shall live by faith.

2. Weeping may endure for the night but joy comes in the morning.

3. The dawning of a new day finds lost hope alive.

4. The darker the night, the nearer the day.

5. The Word of God must accomplish whatever it was sent to do.

6. Drop your needs, worries, and burdens at the feet of Jesus.

7. I can do all things through Christ who strengthens me.

8. God will never leave me or forsake me.

9. Throughout history, Jesus failed no one and He will not begin with me.

10. With great confidence, I rest my case with Jesus.

11. Winners never quit and quitters never win.

12. Never give up on the brink of your miracle.

13. Christ in me IS the hope of glory.

14. Through prayer, pursue, overtake and recover all.

15. Praising God for who He is and for all He has done will cause the walls of Jericho in my life to crumble.

16. Rejoice in the Lord always; again I say rejoice.

17. Put more efforts on your strengths than on your weaknesses.

18. Sharpen your sword to get effective results.

19. Renew your mind for a new vision.

20. Jesus Christ – the same yesterday, today and forever.

21. God is not a man that He should lie, nor the son of man that He should repent, and so I put my trust in Him.

22. If God says it, I can count on it.

23. Give no man permission to reduce you.

24. Do not allow your heart to be troubled, you have a very big God who is always by your side.

25. Arise and shine for your light has come and the glory of the Lord is risen upon you.

26. Be bold and be strong for the Lord your God is with you.

27. Never remain in the place of defeat. Arise and dust yourself off and face the situation, for you are more than a conqueror.

28. You were born and destined to win.

29. I must first be free in order to set the captives free.

30. Never lose hope, for Christ in you is the hope of glory.

31. The joy of the Lord is my strength.

32. Jesus is the Son of God and He is able to carry me through.

33. I will not need to fight in this battle, for the battle is the Lord's.

34. Pursue the enemy, overtake him and recover all your stolen possessions.

35. God is bigger than all your problems

36. Let God alone be exalted in your situation.

37. No weapon formed against me shall prosper.

38. Because God's Word cannot return to Him void; it must bring accomplishment to your life.

39. God loves me so much that He sent His only begotten Son Jesus to die for me.

40. Don't let your heart be troubled. Be of good cheer, for Christ has overcome the world.

41. Be still and know that He is God.

42. Greater is He that is in us than he that is in the world.

43. God will overturn, overturn and overturn whoever is occupying your place until you -- the one whom the crown fits – shall come to wear it.

44. The Lord reigns, and so let your enemies tremble and bow down completely.

45. Let God arise and His enemies be scattered.

46. I can face tomorrow because God lives.

47. What the Lord says and does in your life is permanent.

48. God can never let you down, fail you, or disappoint you. He can only lift you up and take you to the place of your destiny.

49. If God be for us, who can be against us?

50. I am safe because He is my rock, my cleft and my hiding place.

51. Be confident of this very thing: He who has begun a good work in you shall continue to perform it until the day of Jesus Christ.

52. Be convinced that neither life, nor death, nor power, nor might, nor height, nor depth nor perils, nor any difficult situation has the ability to separate you from God's love.

53. You are a peculiar people, a chosen generation and a royal priesthood, so do not feel worthless.

54. Settle for nothing less than what God has for you.

55. The God that answers by fire is alive and He is my God.

56. Let every mountain in my life be removed and be cast into the sea.

57. The Lord God is good and His mercies endure forever, even to all generations.

58. God can do any miracle again and again.

59. The peace of God is mine. I will not be afraid or allow my heart to become troubled.

60. Obey God and eat the good of the land

CHAPTER 6 - Your Kind of Vision
Holding on

The kind of vision you dream about and think of in your heart matters a lot and will go a long way to influence the type of things you create. This is probably the way it is with God's kind of vision, which is certainly always a good one. It is important to be careful of the vision you aspire to give birth to. If you dream small, you will only have the capacity to deliver small. But if you see far and dream big and have faith in the Word of God for it, then you can and will have it. In the Bible, it says that Joseph had a dream of being great and he eventually became great.

Genesis 37:1-11 says:

"And Jacob dwelled in the land wherein his father was a stranger, in the land of Canaan.

> *This is the history of Jacob. Joseph, being seventeen years old, was feeding the flock with his brothers. And the lad was with the sons of Bilhah and the sons of Zilpah, his*

father's wives; and Joseph brought a bad report of them to his father.

Now Israel loved Joseph more than all his children, because he was the son of his old age. Also he made him a tunic of many colors. But when his brothers saw that their father loved him more than all his brothers, they hated him and could not speak peaceably to him.

And Joseph dreamed a dream, and he told it his brethren: and they hated him yet the more.

And he said unto them, Hear, I pray you, this dream which I have dreamed:

Now Joseph had a dream, and he told it to his brothers; and they hated him even more. So he said to them, "Please hear this dream which I have dreamed: There we were, binding sheaves in the field. Then behold, my sheaf arose and also stood upright; and indeed your sheaves stood all around and bowed down to my sheaf."

And his brothers said to him, "Shall you indeed reign over us? Or shall you indeed have dominion over us?" So they hated him even more for his dreams and for his words.

Then he dreamed still another dream and told it to his brothers, and said, "Look, I have dreamed another dream. And this time, the sun, the moon, and the eleven stars bowed down to me."

So he told it to his father and his brothers; and his father rebuked him and said to him, "What is this dream that you have dreamed? Shall your mother and I and your brothers indeed come to bow down to the earth before you?" And his brothers envied him, but his father kept the matter in mind.

In the laws of creation, you are only able to do the much or little that you dream of. If you search the scriptures, you will find out that you can achieve great purpose if only you can dare to believe what it says. So dream big so that your goals can be realised.

LORD, LET ME HAVE A DREAM

Joseph caught his vision, dreamed about it and held on to it until it became a part of him and eventually came to pass. This is how we are supposed to hold on to our vision – tenaciously through prayer, through patience, and through meditating on God's Word until it becomes a part of us and eventually is realized.

As a matter of fact, Joseph was a great man and rich in wisdom from the moment he caught the vision of becoming greater than his brothers, and he was not afraid to tell them about it. This premature announcement caused him untold hardship, as it caused his brothers to hate him. They even tried to kill him, but decided later to sell him into slavery. While Joseph was in Potiphar's house in Egypt, even though God's favor was upon him, he was thrown into prison because he refused to commit adultery with his master's wife. He knew that a man with so great a vision should not sin against God, otherwise the vision could be aborted. He knew that he had been set apart for a divine purpose, and he later accomplished that purpose when he was sent to

Egypt ahead of the time that his family would arrive to deliver them during famine there. Take note that the very moment he knew his purpose on earth, Satan began to trouble him on every side. Joseph conquered every problem until he was released from prison and became the prime minister of Egypt. The same is possible with you in a foreign land or in your own country. You could rule if you will walk in the principles of faith in God, knowing that all things are possible with Him and that all things work together for your good (Romans 8:28).

> *"And we know that all things work together for good to them that love God, to them who are the called according to His purpose."*

In the story about Joseph, the lesson to be learned is that we should be careful about who we share our vision with, because all around us are discouragers and vision-killers who do not want us to rise or to prosper. Remember that there is a time to speak and a time to be quiet. Many people's problems begin when they open their mouth and begin to share their dreams and aspirations with others. Even if that is the situation that you find yourself in right now, just hold on tightly to that dream of greatness, as

Joseph did, and your dream will not die. Do not allow pressure make you settle for less or for smaller things. But as you read this book, I encourage you to go back to that great vision, hold on to it tightly. Embrace it and it will come to pass.

WHERE IS YOUR BOAZ?

In the book of Ruth, we are made to understand that Ruth's mother-in-law, Naomi, decided to return home to her country of Bethlehem-Judah after ten years of living in a sinful city called Moab, where she had lost her husband and two sons. She realized that she missed her vision or the will of God for her by going to the godless nation of Moab during famine. It was now time to go back to Israel.

Naomi caught a fresh vision. Ruth wasted no time in catching her own vision too – one of why she was being formed. One of why she had stuck with her mother-in-law all these years. Ruth knew that she, too, had to seize the opportunity immediately by insisting on following Naomi back to Israel, even though she did not know why.

But the greatness of her dreams on the inside of Ruth gave her the determination to insist, persist and push towards this new dimension and toward new creative abilities. She set her heart faithfully towards the goal of being a winner, and in due time she met and married Boaz. She had a son called Obed, who was the father of Jesse, who was the father of David. And behold! This is the earthly lineage of our Lord and Savior Jesus Christ, the King of Kings and the Lord of the whole universe (see Ruth 4:13-22). What a great vision that was for Ruth to hold on to. She would have missed the greatest blessing and opportunity of her lifetime if she had lost sight of her vision – if she had turned back. But she refused to let go and held tightly onto it until it was fulfilled.

You may have a godless background just as Ruth did. But you could still turn your world around and change your circumstances if you would only invite Jesus into your life. Ask Him to be your Lord and personal Saviour and things will begin to change for the good of all around you. As you begin to exercise faith, your goals will surely come to pass.

Romans 10:9-10 says:

> *"That if thou shall confess with thy mouth the Lord Jesus, and shall believe in thine heart that God hath raised Him from the dead, thou shall be saved. For with the heart man*

believeth unto righteousness; and with the mouth confession is made unto salvation."

Long before young David became a king, he knew that he was made to see and to perform signs and wonders, and that he could kill Goliath. Even when his family and others thought that he could not do it and tried to discourage him, he ignored them and went to face Goliath. He believed in the strength that was on the inside of him and he stood firm without a doubt. Goliath could not intimidate him by his height or his statue. David was not moved by Goliath's uniform, his armor, his previous war experience, his age, his boasts or threats. For David, it was only a matter of putting his faith to action. As he did that, David fortified himself. He killed Goliath with a stone and a sling, and he did it in the name of the Lord.

I want you to be encouraged and not to let any harassment of any kind, or mountains of any sort or any size, make you lose the great vision that is before you. Allow your faith in the Word of God to provoke you and lead you to overcome your circumstance in His time. God will make you an achiever like Himself and you will come out victorious. Do not let family or friends discourage you from attaining your goal. Stand firm in faith, just as David did.

Recently, the Holy Spirit gave me an illustration of a man who had a dream of owning a beautiful house. He set out to build and he began to put all the materials and items he would need in place. Work commenced, but there emerged different problems and difficulties at various stages of the work. As a result, he became frustrated and discouraged. At some stages, his frustration was more than at others, because some structures are more difficult to build...or perhaps more money was involved in some areas such as the foundation, the terrace or the roof.

The Holy Spirit said that this man should keep building and that he should focus on how the house would look in the end. As he would continue to overcome all the obstacles, eventually the building of the house would be completed and fully painted. It would be so beautiful, and his dreams would finally be realized.

What does this mean to us? It means not to try to overcome all your obstacles at once when you're feeling the weight of the world on your shoulders. Overcome each hindrance and each problem one by one – overtaking each one as it comes, while you are creating and building the dream that God has given you. Your miracles will come at the end, and they will be beautiful. And the eyes of all the onlookers will know that God helped you, just as all eyes will see the structure that God enabled that man to build. So do not be discouraged at any stage in your life when you're on your pathway to destiny. If your life begins to resemble an obstacle course, remember, you can overcome every hurdle one at a time.

Jesus refused to be distracted by all the problems, pain and shame that He experienced when He was working on earth, and especially when He was on the Cross. He did not give up on His mission to save the world, but He stuck to His vision and eventually brought salvation to mankind. That is how each one of us should be -- like Jesus – holding firmly to our dream, no matter what we have to go through. Let us be like the diamond, which is a piece of coal that stuck to its job. When it was being refined and enduring very high pressure, it turned out to become something shining, something beautiful. Each of us has a different struggle in life that puts us under pressure like the coal that sticks to a diamond that is being refined. You must stick to your dream. Allow God to refine you and you will become as beautiful as any diamond -- shining toward your destiny.

CHAPTER 7 - Submission
A Mark of Total Surrender for Miracles to Flow

Do not think for one moment that you are too young or too old, too big or too small to be used of God. You are not here on the earth to be a spectator, but to be a co-worker with God. Surrender to Him and allow Him to use you to bring His Word to pass as He did in the life of Prophet Jeremiah. At first, Jeremiah told God that he was a child – as though God didn't already know that. But as God began to encourage Jeremiah, Jeremiah stopped resisting (chapter 1:6-7):

> *"Then said I, Ah, Lord God! Behold, I cannot speak: for I am a child. But the Lord said unto me, Say not, I am a child: for thou shalt go to all that I shall send thee, and whatsoever I command thee thou shalt speak."*

In the book of Judges, Gideon complained. In Exodus, Moses, gave the excuse that he had a speech impediment. Jonah, in the book by his name, had his own reasons why he should not go to Nineveh to preach and set the people free from their sins. He was adamant about not doing God's will and ran away to hide. For three days, Jonah behaved as though he was hiding from God, but he *couldn't* hide from Him, and neither can you or I, no matter where we go. So learn to quickly submit to the Lord, so that you will not delay your blessings and suffer untold hardships due to your disobedience.

Do not doubt God as He leads you and begins to instruct you, because unbelief will hinder the flow of miracles in your life. Remember where Zacharias doubted God when the angel Gabriel had said that he and Elizabeth were going to have a child in their old age? It was because they had been childless all their lives that Zacharias could not fathom that what the angel was saying could actually come to pass. When he began to express words of unbelief, He was made dumb –unable to speak – until the child was born (Luke 1:18-20).

Even Mary the mother of Jesus asked the angel Gabriel how she could become pregnant when she hadn't ever been intimate with a man. The angel encouraged her and told her that the power of the Holy Ghost would overshadow her. Eventually, she submitted to the will of God. (*Read Luke 1:26-35.*) God has called us to work for Him. If He can provide what a virgin needs to conceive, surely will provide all that we need, even against all odds.

Submission
Submitting to God will change your circumstances for the best, but if you resist, you will make a mess of your life. You will begin to feel useless and then begin to question your worth and your purpose. Eventually, Satan will rob you of all the blessings that you were destined to have – not because he has the power to do that in and of himself, but because *you* empower him when you lose your confidence. He will rob you of the blessing that you were destined to be, and the blessings that you were destined to *have*. Our God is a God of grace and mercy. He is also a God of opportunity, and where there isn't one, He will create one. Right now, God is offering you a chance to repent and to focus on Him. Regain your vision and walk in the path that He foreordained for you. Jesus Christ submitted to the will of God for you so that this would not be as difficult. He bore every pain and overcame every obstacle, and He refused to be distracted. He did it all for you and for me. Now you and I, and the whole world can confess Him as Lord and Saviour and be reconciled to God the Father (Hebrews 12:2):

"Looking unto Jesus the author and finisher of our faith; who for the joy that was set before him endured the cross, despising the shame, and is set down at the right hand of the throne of God."

Humble yourself to the course of God in your life and submit to His will (1 Peter 5:5-7).

"Likewise, ye younger, submit yourselves unto the elder. Yea, all of you be subject one to another, and be clothed with humility: for God resisteth the proud, and giveth grace to the humble. Humble yourselves therefore under the mighty hand of God, that he may exalt you in due time: Casting all your care upon him; for he careth for you."

Only when we surrender ourselves and our weaknesses to God can He use us for His purpose. Only then can He gradually begin to perfect us in the area of our particular call for service to the Body of Christ (Ephesians 5:21).

> *"Submitting yourselves one to*
> *another in the fear of God."*

Submitting to one another and, above all, to God is very important. The person you are not cooperating with may be the one God put in your life to lead you to your destiny. We can learn a lot and gain a lot when we submit to one another. But first, we must submit to God. After submitting to God, He might put someone in our lives – a spouse, children, friends, neighbours – who will help accelerate our vision and bring it to pass.

You can be sure that someone is depending on you in one way or another to reach their destiny. And, we should consider it a privilege to be a channel or a blessing to someone – whether they are saint or sinner. We may be very close to God, but let us remember that we are here on earth to be a blessing to all. So, it is important to faithfully submit to the authority of God, and not to Him only, but to the church, to our employers, and to the law!

A submissive heart is a humble heart. Generally, that person is ready to carry out any assignment that is given to him. Consider the parable of the Talents, told by Jesus in Mathew 25: 14-30: A man was traveling to a far country and gave one of his servants five talents. To another servant, he gave two, and to another one, he gave one – all according to their own abilities. The servants who each had 5 and 2 talents obeyed their master. They traded their money and each made a profit by doubling their talents. But the servant that had one talent hid it and did nothing with it. He felt his lord was wicked – that he was reaping where he had not sown, and so he decided not to do anything with his talent.

When their lord came, he welcomed those that made use of their talents into his kingdom and he gave them more talents. From the servant who did nothing with his one talent, he took the talent and gave it to the one that already had 10, and he threw the unprofitable servant into outer darkness.

Will that be you?

God created us with gifts for different purposes, and if we are submissive to Him and to one another and lay aside all excuses and the fear that brings them, we will be able to do greater things than Jesus did and live a fulfilled life.

It is dangerous to be rebellious; it can deprive us of achieving our purpose. It can destroy us. An example of this was when King Saul and the Israelites killed the Amalekites, as commanded by the Lord. The king was commanded to destroy everyone and everything. He didn't obey, though, and he spared King Hagag, he spared the best of the sheep, and oxen and lambs, and everything that he considered to be good. He was motivated by greed. This angered God. Through the Prophet Samuel, God told King Saul that because he rebelled against God, the kingdom had been taken from him and he had been rejected from being king. After this incident, an evil spirit entered Saul and troubled him, and it caused him to be jealous of David. He wanted to kill him.

First Samuel 18:10 says:

> And it came to pass on the morrow, that the evil spirit from God came upon Saul, and he prophesied in the midst of the house: and David played with his hand, as at other times: and there was a javelin in Saul's hand.

When we rebel against God, we open the door to evil spirits. We license them to come into our lives and torment us. The works of the flesh, such as envy, jealousy, and pride will come in where there was none. Unwittingly, we welcome thoughts of lust and the desire to destroy and kill. All these will stop us from fulfilling the purposes that God designed for us.

King Saul was carried away with offering sacrifices to God the way he wanted to. He wanted to offer sacrifices that God did not want. Many people are living this way, and it's the reason why they remain in the same position of unfruitfulness for many years, never advancing in anything. There are some Christians who do a work *for* God but don't work *with* God. They may regularly attend church services, and may be faithful workers in the church. They may speak in tongues, and may be an avid Bible student. But their hearts are still unregenerate. There is no way to have a life that is pleasing to the Lord if you are not submissive to Him. They live in habitual sin -- not of commission, but of omission. They might not be intentionally doing something sinful, but they are omitting to do the one thing that the Lord has asked. Or, they are doing that one thing but in their own way – as did King Saul.

You can only say you are doing God's will if you are doing it His way. To do what God has told you any other way than like He said to do it is a waste of time. To be sure, you will reap the fruit of it, for it pays to sin…but the wages is death (Romans 6:23). Disobedience will bring pain, not fulfilment. Remember, God looks at the heart and He knows when those who work for Him have pure motives. God cannot be fooled. Only a fool thinks He can.

> *"Be not deceived; God is not mocked: for whatsoever a man soweth, that shall he also reap. For he that soweth to his flesh shall of the flesh reap corruption; but he that soweth to the Spirit shall of the Spirit reap life everlasting"* Galatians 6:7-8

Learn to submit to the Holy Spirit. He will lead us without fail to our destiny. There may be decisions you're about to make right now that you know that are not God's will. I command you, by the power of God, STOP. It is better to let God's perfect will take place in your life than what has been called His permissive will. God's will is like his Way: Perfect. So, anything other than God's perfect will is not His permissive will. In fact, it is not His will at all.

The *Permissive* Will?

The consequences of disobeying God is what has become known today as God's *"permissive will."*

To expand on this alleged extension of God's will, let's go through scripture.

God created Adam in His own image, so Adam was supposed to live forever. God told Adam not to eat of the fruit of the tree of the Knowledge of Good and Evil. In Genesis 2, God said to Adam: *"Thou shalt not eat of it."* Adam disobeyed. He ate and received a death sentence. God said that Adam would return to the ground from whence he had come.

Was eating the fruit the "permissive will of God" for Adam?

And let's look in the book of Jonah, named after the prophet, who also disobeyed:

> *"Now the word of the LORD came to Jonah the son of Amittai, saying, "Arise, go to Nineveh, that great city, and cry out against it; for their wickedness has come up before Me." But Jonah arose to flee to Tarshish from the presence of the LORD. He went down to Joppa, and found a ship going to*

Tarshish; so he paid the fare, and went down into it, to go with them to Tarshish FROM THE PRESENCE OF THE LORD."

Even if you do not like what God wants you to do, do not resist. Obey and receive God's free-flowing grace to see you through. It will work out for good if you obey. You will be running from God, thinking you are fleeing "the presence of the Lord," as Jonah did, if you do anything other than God's will.

Was running from God His "permissive will" for Jonah? Was endangering the lives of the other mariners God's will at all (1:4-5)? Was it the *permissive will* of God for Jonah to spend three days and nights in the belly of the "great fish" (v.17)?

None of this was the "permissive will of God." They disobeyed, and they reaped what they sowed. They sowed to the flesh and of the flesh they reaped corruption, just as it says will happen in Galatians 6:8.

CHAPTER 8 - Prayer, Persistence and Patience

We must not undermine our prayers if we want to see the power to create at work in us. Prayer, persistence and patience are intertwined. You cannot separate them if you want to see the power of God manifested in your life. When you persist in prayer, then you must be patient and wait for the answer.

In Ezekiel 37, when God took the Prophet in the spirit to the valley that was full of dry bones, he asked him if those bones could live again. Ezekiel answered by saying, Lord, only You know the answer to that (*paraphrase*). God told Ezekiel to speak life to the bones. The prophet did so and the skeletons were joined together and flesh came on them. Then, the prophet breathed on them and they became alive. God then told Ezekiel to tell the Israelites that even though their bones were dry and their hope was lost, He was going to revive and restore them.

This applies to us too. God wants us to continually release His living power – release it on our problems and in every difficult situation where we find ourselves. God wants us to dwell in His presence daily, praying and interceding for others.

And, when things seem very good with us and around us, we must not take God and His grace for granted.

It appears that Ezekiel listened intently and waited patiently. The miracle unfolded in stages, so he could have become overly excited just at seeing bones joined together. He could have left the scene then, with only half a testimony. But, praise God, he waited and heard God, and in the next stage, He told him to breathe life into the bones. Ezekiel did this and they started moving around. They became a mighty army.

Many of us become satisfied and comfortable with little blessings, or few blessings. We become excitedly noisy with a mere fraction of what God has planned to do through us. Learn to go through every stage with God. Do not leave the scene before the miracle has been completed. We are supposed to experience something new from God at every stage of our lives. Look for fresh manna

In Luke 18:1-8, there was a widow who needed help from a very austere judge – one that didn't fear anyone – God or man. The woman persisted, going before him many times to ask a favor. Finally, the judge responded because he had grown weary of her visits. God loves us so much that we don't need to keep praying over and over for the same things. God is not hard of hearing and He's not slow to move. He has a perfect plan for all those who will rely on Him totally and completely. And, when it seems that our situation isn't changing fast enough, the confidence that we have in Christ is our victory. Your confidence in Christ will produce victory for you.

> And this is the confidence that we have in him, that, if we ask any thing according to his will, he heareth us: And if we know that he hear us, whatsoever we ask, we know that we have the petitions that we desired of him" 1 John 5:14-15

Scripture says that if we ask *anything* in His name, He will do it. Now, asking "in His name" means asking according to His will, and you cannot pray in faith for something that is *not* His will. You must KNOW, not just believe – that what you are praying and believing for is aligned with the Word and the will of God; there can be no faith otherwise. Where would you get that faith from? Certainly not from God, because He won't work against Himself.

Place a demand on God in prayer. But instead of God demonstrating His power to work the miracle, He just might give you the mandate to create your own miracle using the power that is in *you*. Remember, you have *in you* the same power that raised Jesus from the dead. Just remember to be patient, for the vision could be for an appointed time. But Scripture says that if there is delay, wait for it. Do not worry, for it will surely come.

Habakkuk 2:3 says it this way:

> *"For the vision is yet for an appointed time, but at the end it shall speak, and not lie; though it may tarry, wait for it; because it will surely come, it will not tarry."*

Learn to wait in God's presence until something happens. Impatience is the spoiler of destiny and great achievements.

At Gilgal, King Saul and the people of Israel waited for the Prophet Samuel to perform sacrifices to God. But, because of a week's delay in Samuel's arrival, King Saul hastily performed the sacrifice himself because the Philistines were gathered against them and the people were departing from him. Samuel eventually arrived. He rebuked him and told him that the kingdom was no longer established in his house (1 Samuel 13 vs. 1-14). If only he had waited a little longer, Samuel would have performed the sacrifice himself but Saul gave in to pressure and sinned against God just to please the people.

It is better to please God than man. Are you a people pleaser?

There is no excuse for impatience and no benefit in it. You cannot go ahead of God, and you cannot make Him hurry. Disobedience can rob you of your destiny as in 1 Samuel 15:22

> *"And Samuel said, Hath the Lord as great delight in burnt offerings and sacrifices, as in obeying the voice of the Lord? Behold, to obey is better than sacrifice and to hearken than the fat of rams".*

WAIT ON THE LORD
Be encouraged to wait upon the Lord (Psalm 27 vs. 14).

> *"Wait upon the Lord: be of good courage, and he shall strengthen thine heart: wait, I say, on the Lord."*

When I was in Africa, a woman of God told us how she and her pastor-husband travelled to Europe for a few weeks and stayed with their pastor-friend. While there, they had not made any special plans to celebrate her husband's birthday. That day, their host invited them to go shopping. They agreed and climbed into the car with the host, but he obviously had no destination in mind, but drove them from one place to another. The woman whispered to her husband that she wondered what was wrong with him, as he had been driving them around for about one and a half hours without even stopping to go into any of the shops.

At long last, he took them back home and led them to his garden. To their surprise, they saw a crowd partying and they all shouted "Happy Birthday!" The couple entered and were so surprised that they thought it was their host's birthday party. They told him that he should have informed them so they could have bought him a card. The host told them that the party was not for him but for them. He said he took them out only to enable the others to organize the surprise party. This woman said she learned a lesson from that. At the same time that it seemed the host was wasting their time taking them virtually nowhere, he was preparing a feast for them.

This story may describe your present situation. It may seem as if God is taking you round and round, but nothing seems to be happening. Be patient , for God may be preparing a feast for you. Once you see what God has planned for you in the way of blessings, you will be eternally grateful that you allowed Him to work out the best both *for* you and *in* you.

Do not quit now or run ahead in haste. Do not even think of giving up on your dreams. God says that His Word will not return to Him void. On a regular basis, angels take the words we speak and go forth to search out our miracles (Isaiah 55:11). So, speak forth the Word into your situation – whatever it is. It might take some time for you to see the answers to your prayers, but be assured that the answer has always been in Christ. Thousands of years ago, it was in Him on Calvary's Cross. He didn't forget to do anything ahead of time that you would need today.

So, even in challenging times, you need to wait because you might leave at the very time that the spoken word is handling your miracles and is on its way back to you. Your blessings are meant and *sent* to overtake you. You don't want them to find that you have left your position of faith, or that you have given up hope. You don't want to miss receiving your answer. For your purposes to be fulfilled, you must remain in your position. You have to be in a faithful state of expectancy. During the waiting period, be not idle, but fill the vacuum or void by doing something meaningful... for God *and* for someone else.

MARK THE PERFECT MAN

Jesus Christ is our perfect example. He was always fasting and praying and afterwards was able to do miracles, cast out demons and overcome temptations. In order for some situations to change, praying along with fasting is necessary. (*See Matthew 17:21.*)

> *"Howbeit this kind goeth not out but by prayer and fasting."*

As long as we are here on earth, we are in a continuous spiritual warfare. We need to fast and pray to be able to destroy the plans of the wicked and to fulfil our purpose here on earth.

2 Corinthians 10:4 says:

> *"For the weapons of our warfare are not carnal, but mighty through God to the pulling down of strong holds."*

Make use of every available opportunity while your goal is yet to be realised. Gain more knowledge and acquire more skills during the waiting period. Take computer classes or degree courses. Do vocational work, like clothes design or catering. Do volunteer work, take language courses – just do anything you can, at that time, to improve yourself. After all, we know that knowledge isn't lost, and experience acquired and lessons learned will prove to be helpful at some time.

I know a gentleman who was an electronics engineer in europe but had no job. Somehow he learned of a computer training sponsorship offered by a company in the community where he was living. He went for the interview and was accepted and sponsored for a period of time. Immediately after he completed the training, he got a good job and has had many good jobs for years now. I also know of a nurse who was doing fashion design as a hobby. She later left the nursing profession and became a designer full time and really prospered in that area. I know of another nurse who also left her profession and went into full-time church work with her pastor-husband and was doing very well.

The time you spend waiting for a purpose to be fulfilled could lead to a great breakthrough in your life if you occupy yourself positively, meaning become busy doing things that make a positive difference in others' lives. You could start documenting daily happenings of your life in a diary or journal. Who knows? someday you might publish it and become a writer.

The Shunammite woman took care of Prophet Elisha and his servant Gehazi each time they were in her city. She had been barren, but one day Elisha prayed that she would have a child. She had the miracle child, but a few years later the child died. The Shunammite woman did not worry. She made up her mind that all was well with herself and her family. She knew that God could raise up her son and she refused to give up hope. She pressed in to the Lord with urgency. Her faith took action immediately by going to call the Man of God to pray for her son. He prayed and her son was raised up from the dead. (II Kings 4:8-37.)

If everything around you seems dead, and it seems you missed your purpose in life, keep telling your soul and everyone around you that *it is well.* Look unto God for His resurrection power.

In verse 20, the shunamite woman did not need to have left her sick child for that long on her knees until he died before she took action by laying him on the bed of the man of God and running off to call him. The Holy Spirit of God with His wisdom lives in us today to help us make the right decisions at the right time, so we do not suffer untold hardships. Do not allow your situation to go from bad to worse before you begin to seek the face of God or ask for help. But then, even if your situation does worsen, the resurrection power that raised up Lazarus – and Jesus – is able to bring your purpose back to life.

Remember that you are already a winner by the blood of Jesus Christ. No matter how tough the situation is that you are going through, stick to your goal like Jesus did and don't let anything distract you.

Romans 8:35- 39 says:

> "Who shall separate us from the love of Christ ? Shall tribulation, or distress, or persecution, or famine, or nakedness, or peril, or sword?

> "As it is written, for thy sake we are killed all the day long; we are accounted as sheep for the slaughter,

> "Nay, in all these things we are more than conquerors through Him that loved us.

> "For I am persuaded, that neither death, nor life, nor angels, nor

principalities, nor powers, nor things present, nor things to come,

"Nor height, nor depth, nor any other creature, shall be able to separate us from the love of God, which is in Christ Jesus our Lord."

CHAPTER 9 - Meditation
A way to the power house of God

Meditation means reading the Word of God over and over again, followed by reflecting on what has been read until it gets deep into your spirit. Meditation is focusing your thoughts on the Word of God and thinking deeply about what you read or what you heard. It is very important to every believer who wants their purpose to be fulfilled to spend some time daily, if only for a few minutes, meditating on God's Word. It will provide a better understanding of God and His Word. It will also motivate, encourage, and transform your life and more importantly, you will be more apt to demonstrate power from heaven for an effective change in your situation.

Joshua 1: 7-8 says:

> *"Only be thou strong and very courageous, that thou mayest observe to do according to all the law, which Moses my servant commanded thee, turn not from it to the right hand or to the left, that*

thou mayest prosper whithersoever thou goest.

"This book of the law shall not depart out of thy mouth, but thou shall meditate therein day and night, that thou mayest observe to do according to all that is written therein, for then thou shalt make thy way prosperous, and then thou shalt have good success."

In our daily lives, it is very important to set aside a lot of time to study and meditate on the Word of God day and night. We should be more than fond of the Word; we should crave it. We should speak it, live it, eat it, drink it, bathe in it, and dance in it. We should rejoice in it, laugh in it, drive in it, sleep in it, walk in it and swim in it over and over and over again. At the slightest opportunity, let the Word of God surround you. Read it aloud to yourself, and hold it in your heart until it has affected every area of your life.

Do you realize that during meditation, your vision is being broadened? It's the time when God Himself will open your eyes to see solutions to problems that you may have been struggling with for some time. Meditation helps to straighten and strengthen your mind and your heart. You need to realize that a stable heart almost magnetically attracts revelation and insight from God to achieve different purposes. So, do not become too busy to spend quiet time in God's presence. It just might be the answer to your destiny. Make sure you do away with noise and every form of distraction, and prayerfully concentrate. Some writers, like myself, will tell you that when we develop a quiet spirit and reflect on the Word of God imaginatively, ideas and messages flow with such great speed that it can hardly be comprehend or reduced to writing. The ideas come so fast that you have to deliberately take a break.

When you don't spend time meditating on the Word of God, ideas will come, but they will be so dry, in comparison, and there won't be much power or anointing, and that is what transforms.

Psalm 4:4 says:

> *"Stand in awe, and sin not, commune with your own heart upon your bed, and be still."*

It is indeed important to begin your day worshiping God. Pick up the Bible and read a scripture. Begin to meditate on it right then, until your whole being responds to it and is affected by it.

Isaiah 44:6-8 says:

> *"Thus says the Lord, the king of Israel and his redeemer the Lord of hosts; I am the first and I am the last and beside me there is no God*
>
> *"And who, as I, shall call and shall declare it and set it in order for me, since I appointed the ancient people? and the things that are coming and shall come, let them show unto them.*
>
> *"Fear ye not, neither be afraid; have not I told thee from that time and have declared it? Ye are even my witnesses. Is there a God beside me? Yea, there is no God; I know not any."*

This scripture really helped me when I was going through trials. Each time I would meditate on it, I would get a renewed confidence and assurance in Almighty God that nothing could stop me from achieving my purpose on earth. This is because with total authority, God has declared that He is the first and the last. He has thrown an open challenge to anyone to contest it, and *behold!* no one and no power under the heavens or on the earth could do that. This great truth of who God is, is enough of a catalyst to spur us on to greatness. We can know that He is always with us, because He has told us not to be afraid.

Psalm 96:1-3 says:

> *"O sing unto the Lord a new song: sing unto the Lord all the earth. Sing unto the Lord, bless His name; shew forth His salvation from day to day. Declare His glory among the heathen, His wonders among all people."*

Take time – *make* time to praise the Lord and tell Him how great He is. Worship Him and begin to meditate along these lines after. Allow this truth to bubble in your spirit and cause you to proclaim God's wonders and His glory to those around you. There is power in praise and worship, and meditation on His Word can swiftly usher us to our destiny. So read a scripture that speaks to the particular trial that you are going through. Prayerfully reflect and visualize the scene. Savor every word you read and allow the Holy Spirit to open your mind's eye so that you can understand and respond to the Word.

Each time you meditate along a spiritual plane, be sure you reach the height of God's power house, and then see yourself tapping into His power and drawing from it. As you do this, you will soon have the power to begin to create miracles like Him. If the spiritual might and insight that you draw during meditation is applied to your circumstances, by faith, it *will* bring the miracles.

Try meditating on the Word of God from now on and begin to experience a world of difference in learning how to make things happen. Do not always be in a hurry, but give place and time to the study of God's Word and to meditation. You will come to know very well that the difference is clear and incontestable.

CHAPTER 10 - Love
Good ground for miracles

There is power, peace, joy, favour, and God's glory in love. These are all mighty tools with which you can attract and create miracles to change your world. Just as in farming, you need the right texture of soil to grow crops (in addition to other factors), so you need the love of God in your heart as the proper soil for good works to grow in. As you walk with the soil of love in you, there will be no limit to what you can do through Christ.

Consider so great a love when God sent His only begotten Son Jesus to die for the sins of the world, as recorded in John 3:16:

> *"For God so loved the world that He gave His only begotten son, that whosoever believeth in Him should not perish, but have everlasting life."*

God's love toward us prompted Him to give us Jesus, Who loves us and gave His life for us. It was *agape* love for us that brought Him down to the earth. When love shows up and is demonstrated, it gives birth to something good and something miraculous. The soil of love has great potential in the supernatural to do all kinds of good works, and that includes giving birth to your dreams. So love the Lord your God with all your heart. Love your neighbour as yourself. Let the fruit of the Holy Spirit grow in you; one of them is *love*. And as you relate in love to others, the environment will be created for you to fulfil your dreams. In 1 John 4:7, it says:

> *"Beloved, let us love one another, for love is of God, and everyone who loves is born of God."*

A true godly love existed between David and Jonathan, son of King Saul (1 Samuel 19:2-3). And because it did, Jonathan warned David to flee from Jonathan's father Saul, who was planning to kill David. Jonathan knew that David would become the next king if David's life was spared. And even though Jonathan would have become king if David were to die, Jonathan knew that was not the will of God. So, because he loved both God and David, his selfless love sought to protect David's life. Like Jonathan, you should not be afraid to show love, no matter what the sacrifice, because God's reward will be greater. When it comes to showing God's love to others, it does not matter who you are, where you are from, or what your background or profession is. They are irrelevant.

David's life was spared and eventually he became the king of Israel. He loved God, achieved a lot and was a blessing to many. His life and testimonies in the Psalms are available to bless us today because someone loved David enough to protect him from being murdered. That is how love behaves -- it releases people and catapults them into their destinies (1 John 4:18–19).

> *"There is no fear in love, but perfect love casts out fear because fear involves torment, but he who fears has not been made perfect in love. We love him because He first loved us."*

I was privy to another example of God's true love with our late Archbishop Benson Idahosa in Nigeria, of the Church of God Mission International, Inc. As was often told to members of the church, that he was sickly and weak when he was born, so his father gave up hope on him and threw him away in an open dirt heap in their back yard. But his mother, who loved him so much, never gave up on him. She was able to see life in him. She sneaked out and rescued her son, and ran away to take care of him in the village. Months later, when his father visited them, he did not recognize his son, as little Benson now looked well. Benson Idahosa later became a great man of God that blessed many nations.

Some years ago, one Friday morning in my local church in Nigeria, a week-old baby girl was abandoned outside the fence of the church. Her hands and feet were tied together with a baby shawl and she was wrapped in a carrier bag. Our pastor informed the police about this and they made arrangements for the baby to be sent to an orphanage the following Monday. But my mother was living with us and could help look after her, so they lived with my family that weekend. The baby was weak, her cry was faint, and she had ant bites on her body, so my late mother cleaned her, fed her and kept her warm. My two daughters, Faith and Sandra, who were very young, named the baby Glory and they played with her. Her voice became stronger and she was now eating very well and smiling.

My family became so fond of her and so close to her during the initial three days that she was living with us. For a long time, my children always asked after her. The church continued to see her and provide gifts for her until we learned that she had been adopted by a very good family. Her mother had meant for her to die, but through God's miraculous intervention, she was rescued and many different people showed her love at every stage of her life. God had predestined her to live and to fulfil a purpose here on earth. That is what love does; it releases your purpose, as well as the purposes of others. So learn to love and to accept love, and the world will be a better place – a place that is filled with achievers of their destinies. Through this experience, I made a decision to help orphanages and help needy children, because it is good to be a blessing to people and to know that you have played a part in them succeeding in life.

Look around you. Try to find someone who needs your love, your smiles, your time, and your attention. Show a little kindness to someone every day of your life. Do not get tired of doing good for others, because there is satisfaction and peace that comes along with it. Blessing others creates an environment that discharges and sometimes inundates you with divine ideas. It often opens doors of breakthrough in your own life.

God loves you so much that He sent His Son Jesus Christ to lay down His life for you and bless you with the gift of life, a job, good health, family, and material and spiritual gifts. He protects you day and night from all kinds of evil. So let this great love toward you spur you on to love God and those around you. There is no reason why you should feel lonely or unloved or find it difficult to love others.

The love of God toward you is the greatest love you could ever know. Maybe you were rejected by your parents or loved ones, or by someone else. It should not take over your whole life, nor should your feeling unloved determine how far you will go in life. God loves you and He is always there for you. The lack of some things you desire should not cause you to feel lonely and rejected. Instead, you should consider what you *do* have and begin to constantly thank God all the more for that – no matter how much or how little it is. Learn to pray through, no matter what you have or don't have. Allow yourself to see the miracle that being grateful can bring. In the process of waiting for your answer, live in a way that is loving to others and that will have others behaving lovingly to you in return. Learn to celebrate God *and* yourself. Stop hating yourself, but instead, take good care of yourself in every area of your life, because when you are whole, you can be a blessing to others.

When I have said and done things that I should not have, I felt very bad but I had to forgive myself and trust God to help me move past the terrible state that I was in, and He delivered me every time. No matter what you have done, ask for forgiveness and accept the love of God. Don't be hard on yourself, because you cannot move forward except you forgive yourself and love yourself. Unforgiveness and bitterness shut out the ability to create miracles. It is a huge obstacle to fulfilling your destiny, so, learn to forgive others of their faults and offenses.

FORGIVENESS

I had always been able to easily forgive others by excusing their faults and analyzing the reasons why they may have offended me. Before I would get to the tenth reason, I would find the reason to forgive and forget. But years ago, someone offended me, and I analyzed and reanalyzed and could not find any reason why she did what she did to me. Unforgiveness crept into my heart and began to eat away at me. I was so uncomfortable and angry at the mention of her name or anything that had to do with her. I knew this was wrong, but I could not bring myself to forgive her.

After a few months of carrying on in this state, I listened to someone's testimony in the church.

She was a young widow with three children, and she talked about the cruelty her father had shown to her in spite of her predicament. She testified about how she forgave him and how far she went to bring peace between them. My heart was touched. I thought within me that my case was not even as bad as hers. When I got home, I cried out to God to help me and He did. I was set free from bitterness and was able to forgive her. I had peace afterward and related with her in peace. Since then, I have become very careful not to find myself in that state again. For any kind of offence, I just pray about it and ask God to help me forgive and love again.

During a conference some years ago in Nigeria, a visiting bishop gave a testimony of how he was angry with the late Archbishop Benson Idahosa for two years. For this reason, his ministry suffered financially and there were fewer people coming to church. His peace eventually left him and he began to tell other pastors in the country of how Idahosa, the great man of God, had offended him. But he said that a visiting pastor from the United States of America heard about it and rebuked him, and told him to repent because it was foolish for him to carry on like that. He eventually took the good counsel and repented before God, and then went to meet the Archbishop himself and ask for his forgiveness. The Archbishop prayed for him and asked God to prosper him. Later, things changed for good in his life, and his ministry flourished in every area. He later wrote two books on unforgiveness and has been preaching that message from place to place.

In same conference, a Nigerian pastor residing in the United States gave a testimony of how his mother had abandoned him and his father when he was just a few weeks old. So his father brought him up alone, but died when he was five years old. He was taken to the orphanage where the First Lady of the state educated him. He later became a pastor. This first lady had extended her love to many others and had made many dreams come true. We should all learn to give someone else something good that we have on the inside of us. It might just be a hug, a smile, or good and godly counsel. Learn to give in prayer, or give of your time and money. Just make sure you are good to somebody.

There was an incident in my local church in Nigeria whereby a male and a female youth were suspended for 6months because of fornication after they had refused to obey a series of warnings. This meant that they would sit at the back of the church and nobody would be allowed to shake hands with them. Also, they would not be allowed to serve in the church until they had repented. Only then would the ban be lifted up. They both came to the church a few times, but finally stopped coming completely. I was moved with love for them and did a follow-up on them. They stopped the relationship and I encouraged them to write an apology letter to the church. Only the guy did, and he was forgiven and restored back to church. As time went on, he was doing well in the Lord and became an assistant pastor at another church. Each time I remember the incident, it gives me joy and encourages me to invest in other people's lives in every way I can, because it can go a long way to transform them and lead them to their destinies.

CHAPTER 11 - Trials and Temptations
A way to the top

Trials and temptations actually take us one step at a time toward achieving our goals, but often a lot of people do not see it that way. Rather, they think it is meant to destroy them. They remain in a position of defeat and eventually just give up the fight. The scripture says that we should rejoice in hope, and be patient in tribulation, continuing in prayer (Romans 12:12).

James 1:12 says:

> *"Blessed is the man who endures temptation, for when he has been proved, he will receive the crown of life which the Lord has promised to those who love Him."*

Do not fret or be discouraged when difficulties come your way. Instead, strive onto victory like Daniel did. He and the other three Hebrews that we know as Shadrach, Meshach and Abednego were taken captive in Babylon, but they all prospered. God's favor was so much on Daniel that King Darius made him a leader over the other rulers of the land. God gave him revelations and wisdom to help the king and his kingdom. But the ungodly rulers were envious of Daniel and convinced the king to make a decree that no other god should be served except the king himself. They knew that Daniel would surely pray to the God of heavens and this would bring him the death penalty. It was so and he was thrown into the lions den. But God sent His angels to shut the mouths of the lions and Daniel was delivered. The king eventually threw the wicked men and their families into the den of lions. They were all killed and Daniel prospered. Later, the king wrote to all the people and nations a decree that they should all fear the God of Daniel whose dominion shall be unto the end. (Daniel 6).

Daniel said that he would not defile himself with the king's food and wine. He ate only vegetables and drank water and looked better than all those who ate of the king's portions. From the beginning of the book of Daniel you will find that he was faced with different trials and temptations, but he trusted in God and was victorious (Daniel 1:8-14). As Daniel, we also are supposed to resist falling into any form of temptation that comes our way. Whenever we let go of worries, doubt, fear and intimidation, and let God have His way in our lives, trials and temptations will be as a ladder to victory, which is what is promised to us. Learn to trust God at all times especially, in the face of trials and He will take care of you.

Psalms 91:11 says:

> "For He shall give His angels charge over thee, to keep thee in all thy ways."

In trials and tribulations, the common question Christians ask is "Why me? Why did this problem happen to me?" The Bible says in 1 Corinthians 10:13:

> "There hath no temptation taken you but such as is common to man: but God is faithful who will not suffer you to be tempted above that ye are able; but will with the temptation also make a way to escape, that ye may be able to bear it."

God will not allow you to go through trials that will destroy you. Having difficulties in life is not the real problem; it's how we see it and handle it. We should see every trial in life as an opportunity and stepping stone to our success. I encourage you to see things positively. Do not let these problems get to you. Do not cave in and display a chicken's heart that is weak and ready to give up. This kind of heart is afraid to commit to God because it is also afraid to confront adverse situations.

DO NOT ACCEPT DEFEAT

At a time like this, you need the spirit of a lion – bold and strong – one that will fight back no matter what the threat. The lion goes after its prey, fights it and conquers it by force. Even when faced with an armed man, the lion is still bold enough to face him and go after him. It is time you know who you really are –the son of the King. It's time you know that all power belongs to Him and He has empowered you. You were created to dominate, to create, change and rule the world around you.

Do not accept or even entertain failure or defeat. You have cried long enough. Wipe away your tears, jump out of your bed of depression and self-pity, freshen yourself up and pray. Think clearly and walk tall with your shoulders high. There is a time limit for every trial and it cannot exceed its bounds. That's good news. God has placed sand for the bounds of the sea by a perpetual decree so that it cannot pass it. And though the waves toss about to and fro, yet they cannot prevail. Though they roar, they cannot pass over it (Jeremiah 5:22).

Isaac was another man in the Bible who refused to be defeated by his enemies. He was blessed by God and had herds of flock that needed water for their survival. Without it, they would have died and he would have become poor. But he found out in time that years prior, his father Abraham had many wells in that area, but the Philistines had covered them. So he started digging. Each time he dug and found water, the Philistines came fighting for claim again and again, but he refused to be intimidated. He persisted until they finally gave up and left him alone. Genesis 26:12-22:

> Verse 22 *"And he removed from thence, and digged another well; and for that they strove not and he called the name of it Rehoboth; and he said, for now the Lord hath made room for us, and we shall be fruitful in the land."*

The herds were calm and waited patiently for their master Isaac to provide them with water to drink. They knew that he had protected them all along, fed them, and led them through green pastures. They did not scatter and wander away in confusion at the time it took Isaac to sort out the matter. They knew he would not abandon them and it was so. The same way that Isaac's herds needed water, so you need substance, sustenance, and sundry resources – money, love, peace, healing, and so many other things to fulfil your destiny. But you have to trust God, your Master, to fight battles and put food on your table.

As we know, water is very important to man. It refreshes, quenches thirst, and is used for making meals, washing and cleaning. It's used for making all types of mixtures and solutions. And as vital as it was to Isaac, his family and herds, the enemy had taken a step ahead to block the wells and to frustrate his hopes – his source of joy and fulfilment – by making sure that the Philistines took away every well that he had dug. So, the joy and excitement they had by finding water was short-lived and the circle continued until one special day when they strove no more.

This could be your case – you have trouble keeping jobs for very long, or keeping relationships. You heave a sigh of relief when you think one problem has been solved, but before you can enjoy your testimony, one or more serious problems comes up and you continue in frustrating cycle over and over again.

God has blessed us with all good things, but the enemy has gone ahead of us to block them from our reach. We give in and get frustrated and live from hand to mouth, never seeing the wider picture. We tend to forget our dreams and the purpose for which we were born. Be determined not to give up. Stand on the Word of God. Do something new about your dreams every day.

Know that God made provisions for you even before you realized you had a need. It might be that the enemy *has* blocked your blessings, and an area of your life is not bearing fruit. All you need is to recognize the fact that God is good and His promises endure forever. God is not a man that He should lie, nor is He the son of man that he should repent. What He says, He will make good (Numbers 23:19), so hold on to Bible passages that fit your situation. Apply them daily, saying them out loud. Use them as instruments to dig you out of your situation and carve your miracle. No matter how long it takes, make sure you dig out your water from the blocked well, so that the enemy can no longer steal from you.

Some years ago in my country of Nigeria, workers were not being paid regularly. There was great frustration in many families that led to people thinking of other sources of income. It was especially this way in Edo state, where I came from, which was primarily known for white-collar jobs. The people opened all kinds of businesses to augment their income, and things got better. So you see, there is breakthrough and success alongside every trial and temptation, so look deep within yourself. Dig out that solution to your situation just as Isaac strove hard until he made sure he dug out clean water from the well.

The period of trials is not the time to have an unbalanced routine of eating, sleeping, watching television and becoming lazy. You know all the television programs and cannot really do other important things towards your goal in life. It is all right to eat, sleep, watch television and have recreational activities, but do not let these things control your life and tie you down from your main dream. For those of you on state benefits -- do not kill your potential but find something to do *now* that will bring you an income. Live well tomorrow. Do not limit yourself. It is time now to watch and pray until something happens. It is also the time to visit old dreams and dream new ones.

Begin to make notes. Add important things and delete irrelevant ones. Place your dreams in the order of their priority.

No matter what you are going through in life, only you can limit yourself. No one can stop you except you give them the permission and power to do so. You can achieve whatever you set your heart to do.

Most people get discouraged during difficult times, but the truth is that you can only get a breakthrough if you see challenging times as doors of opportunity and courageously walk through them. There are testimonies of some people who were made redundant during the recent global economic crises who opened new businesses and where some other businesses went bankrupt, some existing ones were thriving well and expanded. So ask yourself – what do you see in times of trials? Magnified problems? Fear? Or faith? Solutions? or new oppurtunities? . Resolve within you that if no one encourages you, encourage yourself, because God is on your side and there are more than enough promises in the Bible to lift your spirit. Remember that you are unique and you're the only one in the whole wide world that has your thumbprint; no one else has it. You and your uniqueness have the ability to succeed.

Psalm 139:14 says:

> *"I will praise You, for I am fearfully and wonderfully made; marvelous are Your works, and that my soul knows very well."*

Even in times of troubles, know that you are a marvellous creation of the work of God. Be ready to win all your battles by moving past them to good success. Locate your talents and gifts within, and attune yourself to destiny, because there is room for everyone to shine. I have heard and known of many great people who were so poor and had all manner of problems in their life, but they overcame them by pressing on to greatness.

Study has shown that the eagle soars straight through storms and the air current, toward areas that disturb lesser birds. The eagle has excellent eyesight and can see from far away, and because of their size have few enemies. When you find yourself in the storms of life, with all kinds of problems, just mount up your wings like the eagles. Soar above the problems by rooting yourself in the Word of God. It will frustrate the enemy right out of your life.

Romans 8:31 says:

> *"What shall we then say to these things? If God be for us, who can be against us?"*

THE EYE OF FAITH

Consider how you see things, how far you see, and what you see. Try and look beyond the difficulties. Draw strength from the world around you and the victory ahead that will bless you. Our Lord and Saviour Jesus Christ endured the Cross and looked beyond the shame and pain of His death, seeing far ahead all the way to the joy of the salvation that He was making available to the whole world.

Hebrews 12 verse 2 says:

> *"Looking unto Jesus the author and finisher of our faith, who for the joy that was set before him endured the cross, despising the shame, and is set down at the right hand of the throne of God."*

Do not let your heart faint by accepting defeat, confessing negative words, or becoming passive and walking through life as a failure. Wait upon the Lord your God, as we are exhorted to do in the book of Isaiah 40:31:

"But they that wait upon the Lord shall renew their strength, they shall mount up with wings as eagles, they shall run, and not be weary, and they shall walk, and not faint."

Where there is no job, look for vacancies and prayerfully send your applications until you find one. Whatever the problem is, find a scripture in the Word of God that fits it. Confess that scripture over your life and continuously sow faith seed toward your breakthrough. As Christians, we are spiritual people, so we need to obey spiritual laws and apply them to our situation for deliverance.

Take control over your situation. Make new moves so that God can do something new for you. Stop crying, quit being lazy, and never take *no* for an answer. Do something worthwhile with your life and if need be, go back to school either full-time or part-time to better yourself. Walk tall and see how you can do something different that can make you attain your goal in life.

In case of financial problems, examine your giving to God and to the things of God, ministries, the poor and underprivileged, and others. By faith, increase your offerings and faithfully pay your tithe, no matter how difficult things are with you.

Luke 6:38 says:

> *"Give, and it shall be given unto you, good measure, pressed down, and shaken together, and running over, shall men give into your bosom. For with the same measure that ye mete withal it shall be measured to you again.*

Challenge God by obeying His Word and you will be successful in life. It is the will of God for you to prosper even as his word says in Third John verse 2

> *"Beloved, I wish above all things that that thou mayest prosper and be in health, even as thy soul prospereth."*

As you are reading this book, seize the opportunity, for once in your life, to ignore your problems. Learn to believe God and focus on the solutions. With my experience in life, I know that some problems may take a long time to leave, but while you are praying for answers and after doing all you know to do, lay all your challenges at the feet of Jesus. Move on in the other areas of your life, but at the same time, continue to believe God for change.

The time and duration of trials can be likened to different sowing and harvest seasons for different crops. For example, it takes a shorter time for maize to be planted and harvested than to plant and harvest yam. But with the avocado pear it takes years for it to mature and bear fruit. That is how it is in our lives. Answers to prayers come at varying times and seasons. An answer in one area of your life may come quickly, and in another area it may take a very long time. But understand this and wait for it, because God will release the answer at the right time. As you know very well, it is easier to weed the grass than to cut down a timber tree and root out its stumps and tap roots, because it takes a lot of time and strength to do that. Some problems are like the grass – before you realize it, the solution has come, but some have taproots that require time, patience, wisdom, fasting and prayer and a perfect finish from God to get answers. So see your difficulties as an opportunity for victory to the top, fulfilling your goal in life.

CHAPTER 12 - Assurance

Act fast and rise to the occasion

The earlier you are sure of what your dreams and purposes are, the better it is and will continue to be for you. Once you know, begin to make plans on how to execute them. It is so sad when you see and hear of people procrastinating, saying they will do this or that tomorrow, but end up doing nothing about their dreams. The fact is that you should do something about it as early as you can and as soon as you can and keep your dreams alive by revisiting them every day.

There are some people who live in a dream world without ever coming out of it. It is good to dream but sometime later, bring it to pass in the real world you live in, for without which you would still suffer and live in lack. Others live, talk and act in the past. They talk about the good and the bad things that happened to them yesterday and cannot move on. They say God used them so much years ago, and they used to hear Him audibly and had great fellowship with the Holy Spirit, because He did great miracles in their lives. They could go on and on for years repeating same old stories.

They could also talk about how they were abused at whatever stage of their lives and somehow they just cannot move past it.

This is a very wrong and complicated way to live one's life. You have to know that God has not changed and can still use you today. He can speak to you and heal your heart from hurt. He can help you and do miracles in your life because His power is still the same. Remember, Jesus Christ is the same yesterday, today and for evermore, as it says in Hebrew 13:8. Just as the Apostle Paul did, do away with plaguing thoughts of your past and move on. Try to see the wider picture of why you must succeed.

Philippians 3:13 says:

> *"Brethren, I count not myself to have apprehended but this one thing I do, forgetting those things which are behind, and reaching forth unto those things which are before...."*

As the Holy Spirit plants ideas into your heart, act fast, with confidence, to do what He has asked you to do. Be assured that He is there with you and will remain with you till the end. During the course of writing this book, there were times when I was almost discouraged and started thinking of other options. I kept looking at other Christian authors who did not go really far with their works, and I was comparing the way God was telling me to go with them. But each time, I would hear the Holy Spirit say, "You are Gladys and I am leading you in the way of greatness" and "You are not that other person." I would then be encouraged to go on, and was ready to storm my world with the good things God has deposited inside of me.

In 1 Samuel 17:1–51, there is the story of how young David killed Goliath, even when his brothers and other people could not face the giant. They thought that David could not face him either, and they discouraged him from confronting Goliath. They felt that he had come to complicate matters for the Israelites by showing up on the scene. But when they realized that David was meant to fight with Goliath, they put their traditional army uniform on him, which was too heavy. So, he had to break tradition by taking it off; the armor did not suit him.

David took his sling and five smooth stones and stood before the giant Goliath. He was not intimidated by Goliath's looks, his stature or his war experience, and the mockery didn't faze him at all. David recalled how God had helped him to kill a lion and a bear. He knew that same God who delivered him from being devoured by dangerous animals would also give him victory over Goliath. David taunted Goliath, saying that Goliath was coming to fight him with a sword, a spear and a javelin. But David said that he had come to fight Goliath in the name of the Lord of hosts, whom Goliath had defiled. And true to what David believed, he smote Goliath the Philistine, hitting him in his forehead with a stone. Goliath fell over, and David went right over to him to cut off his head. He wanted to make sure that Goliath would not rise up again against the Israelites. Victory was thereby brought to all.

Just like David, you should be very passionate and very confident about what God wants you to do. Others might not fully understand, because it is your dream, and not theirs. In order to realize these dreams, you may need to ignore or disregard some counsel that you are not comfortable with, no matter who gave it to you. And you may need to break with previously religious traditions to achieve your goal in life.

So, be sensitive to the leading of the Holy Spirit at all times. David had no time to waste asking for prayer or fasting about the situation. The situation was at hand and needed an instantaneous solution. And so it is with us. We have to know the urgency of timely accomplishing our dreams, because many lives and destinies depend on it. One cannot imagine what would have happened to the nation of Israel if David had been timid and not bold to stand for what he believed as his life was at stake. There are many people in the world around us, and even ourselves, who are still in bondage today. We are either timid or confused, and not bold like David to draw strength from the Word of God.

DESTINED TO WIN

Maybe you have a chronic situation that needs a new approach for realizing your breakthrough, but you are afraid of change. Take a bold step of faith right now. Act fast. Jump up and run toward the goal, and do not allow anything or anyone to stop you. The difference between winners and losers is that winners never give up. Even if they fall, they don't fail. A winner is not afraid to try again until something dramatic happens. You fail only when you stop trying. Losers just remain in same position, making excuses for why they cannot do it and try again. They fear the failure to make mistakes, hence they end up never really giving themselves a fair opportunity to prove that they can succeed. That is how they end up as a loser. But God forbid that a Christian give up on success and live a defeated life! Do not settle for less. Do not quit until you conquer all ground that God has given to you.

A winner will keep winning new territories. A loser should rise up right now and begin to win. Do not give up on God. When you give up on God, you have given up on life. I have seen many people who were angry with God in times of trials. Many years ago, there was this sister in Nigeria who was going through difficult times with her loved ones. She stopped going to church and said she was angry with God for allowing those problems to befall her family. Her situation grew worse and as a friend, I kept visiting and encouraging her, but she would deliberately say things to offend me so that I would not come to her again. I did not give up on her until she repented and was restored back to faith. Her family eventually got a great breakthrough beyond their imaginations.

Do what you can do today about your dreams. Do away with sluggishness and laziness. Just for one moment, consider the ways of the ant and learn wisdom from her, as it speaks about in Proverbs 6:6-11. The ant has no ruler or overseer, but is well organized. The ant gathers and stores food in summer and hence, beats the problems of cold, which are not favorable for her. The ant has a time to work, and to rest and to eat all year-round. The lazy person has no excuse but to rise up now. As the ant, plan well and act fast.

It takes wisdom from God to know when and how to act fast. An example is in Judges 15:4-5, when Samson wanted to destroy the fields of the Philistines . He understood that he needed a strategy to get a purposeful result. He needed more creative ideas that would yield results faster than his ability could. Samson got three hundred foxes and tied them tail to tail and set fire in between them. He then released them into their fields, burning down all their crops in a short time. What the foxes did was like using present-day dynamite. Today, we need these same divine ideas as to how to achieve our goals quickly, instead of wasting years on what God has placed a time limit on. Ask God for wisdom to bring about that dream.

James 1: 5 says:

> *"If any of you lack wisdom, let him ask of God, that giveth to all men liberally, and upbraideth not, and it shall be given him."*

THE MAIN THING

It is very frustrating to try to do things on our own without the wisdom of God, because the Bible says that "wisdom is the principal thing" -- or the *most important* thing. It goes on to say that in all our getting, we should get understanding." We need to have a better understanding of our situation and of the changes that we are about to experience

Proverbs 4:7:

> *"Wisdom is the principal thing, therefore get wisdom, and with all thy getting get understanding.*

Let the name of God be glorified in your life by pressing on to victory. Judges 11:1-11 tells of the story of Jephthah who was the son of a harlot. His half-brothers cut him out of his father's inheritance. He fled from them and settled in the land somewhere southeast of the Sea of Galilee. He surrounded himself with those who believed in him and who knew he was a mighty man of valor in spite of his present state. As time went on, his brothers had problems and were threatened by war. They had to approach Jephthah to help them fight. He agreed to do it with the promise that they make him leader over them once the battle had been won. They agreed and he rose to the occasion and trusted God to deliver them. He won the battle and became ruler over them. When they drove him away, it seemed as if he had lost his inheritance, but the God of a second chance gave him another opportunity to do what God had called him to do.

Maybe in your past, you were a prostitute, a drug addict, a murderer. Maybe you were poor, were raised by a single parent, or grew up being sent to different orphanages. It may seem that you are hated by men. It may appear that you are the lowest in society. Perhaps you were cut out of your inheritance. Whatever your story is, do not give up on your dreams.

Luke 1:17 says:

> "...for with God, nothing shall be impossible."

The same people who drove away Jephthah, later came to him for help. So are those mocking you today and giving you a rough time may have to come by you again. They might later be required to rejoice with you. But they might also be required to humble themselves and ask for your help. They will see that you are a winner, for you will surely rule over them. There is a challenge before you right now that you need to deal with without delay. Go for it. Bring it on and win the battle.

You need to know your worth and see yourself as God sees you. You need to have it in your consciousness that you were made in God's image and likeness and can do greater works than Jesus Christ did.

There is a crown of victory that has been taken away from you, but like the crown, your trials are meant to fit you only. In Ezekiel 21:26-27, God says that He will overturn, overturn and overturn until you who the crown fits should come. The crown of victory is in the hand of God and is ready to be placed on your head the moment you take your proper position to depose that impostor, the devil. He has been wearing the crown of your marriage, your job, the peace of your family and relationships. He has worn the crown of your talent, your finances, your success, and all the blessings that God has set aside expressly for you.

God has made every provision for you to pursue, overtake and recover all that the enemy has stolen from you. So do not sit back without doing anything. Do not settle for little or for peanuts. Go and possess all the good things God has for you. You have been made to be more than a conqueror. You are a victor! Why have you settled for years to work for minimum wage without improving on your self-worth?. Do not limit yourself to doing small things, as if you cannot have faith for great ones. The problem in your life is that a thief came to rob you of your joy and testimony. Do not let him stay any longer. This is a time to examine yourself and to make corrections in your life. Prepare to do battle, no matter the trials before you. Face them and deal with them, and make sure you achieve your goal.

CHAPTER 13 - Sin
A Great Hindrance

Sin is a great hindrance to achieving one's goal. It contaminates, destroys, and makes you lose your dream. It finally will separate you from God.

Isaiah 1:19 says:

> *"If you are willing and obedient, you shall eat the good of the land."*

THE WAGES OF SIN
Romans 6:23 says the wages of sin is death.

God has prepared blessings for obedient people. Samson was a great man of God who was sanctified from his mother's womb. But the sin of fornication caused the power of God to leave him without his realizing it until he was betrayed and taken captive by the enemies he had once defeated. But the moment he realized it, he repented of his sin and prayed that God's power would again come on him. Immediately, he was forgiven and had so much power. He was able to destroy his enemies, but he died with them. This is not the best kind of miracle – to die with your enemies. But it was this way with Samson because sin has its reward. It has its consequences, and the consequences are ours to bear, even though we may have been forgiven. (Read Judges 16.)

We are pressed about with all kinds of testimonies of the goodness of God in our lives therefore, let us honour God and do away with every habitual sin that we so easily commit and live holy lives.

Hebrews 12:1:

> *"Therefore my brethren since we are surrounded by every one work of God, let us lay aside every weight and the sin which so easily besets us, and let us run with endurance the race that is set before us."*

You need to do away with habitual sin to achieve your purpose in life. Right now, you may have lost your dreams and visions because of sin. Remember that God loves you and He is a merciful Father. He will forgive you if you repent of your sin, and your dreams will be restored. Beware of sin, because it is like a canker worm and will eat deep into your soul. Eventually, it will spread throughout your whole body like cancer. Except you stop it by repenting, it can kill you. It *will* kill you.

One thing about wilful sin is that although you have repented, the scar will always be there and you may have to learn to live with it if you are to be successful. You can liken this to a person who had a large open sore that got healed. There remains a scar showing that there was once a wound on that part of the body. Samson repented and became a very powerful blind man who died with his enemies. But he did not live to testify about it. This is not the kind of testimony that you or I want. It is better to live and see your victory over your enemies. As a matter of fact, it is a waste of time starting all over again after repenting, but it is better to start again than to remain in that destructive state of sin.

In Luke 22:56-60 tells of how Peter, Jesus' disciple, denied Jesus three times before he was crucified. Peter repented afterwards, and was bold and preached about Jesus Christ to many as recorded in Acts 2:14-41. But this was not so in the case of Judas Iscariot, who betrayed Jesus for money and did not repent but killed himself. You walk the path of death if you fail to repent. This may come in form of spiritual death, or a premature physical death, which leads to eternal condemnation.

Sin can be likened to a poisonous arrow that is ready to pierce your heart to failure and death. Just imagine -- what you think is pleasurable or fun is actually like HIV AIDS that has come to steal your destiny by making your life miserable and eventually killing you. It could also be like drinking a cup of tea daily that contains a deadly substance mixed with sugar or honey, and is coated with milk from your enemy who pretends to be your friend. There is no doubt that this will slowly destroy you, and before you realize it, great harm has been done to your body and your life.

Many people – great men of God – have fallen into all kinds of sin. Fornication, adultery and other sexual sins have caused a minister's world to fall apart, along with his or her great ministry. Some repented and were restored. Others could not forgive themselves. If you are in a similar situation now, repent and start anew. This time, pursue your vision with diligence, for our God is a God who will provide a number of chances.

Some years ago, while walking along a road, the Holy Spirit began to explain to me the reason why so many men and women of God easily fall into sexual sins. He said that because they carry the anointing of God in them, because of the presence of the Holy Spirit in them, their faces and their lives glow with love and peace. And people become attracted to this power of God in them, but the minister gets carried away and misunderstands this. He or she thinks that the people are attracted to them as a person or to their own personality. Instead of relating with these people with the pure love of God, they begin to think that they are so loved. And with their inflated ego, they give in to adultery or fornication.

Be very careful and know that as a Christian, the Holy Spirit dwells in you. Sure, people will become attracted to you because of God's anointing that is on you. So you owe it to God, to yourself, and to the people to relate to everyone with the pure love of God.

Maybe your life is at a standstill right now because of transgressions, or it may be stale and reek of sin. All you need to do is to repent and be converted, and God will touch you. Your life will be refreshed and renewed with His presence.

Acts 3:19 says:

"Repent ye therefore, and be converted, that your sins may be blotted out, when the times of refreshing shall come from the presence of the Lord."

THE CRIMSON STAIN

Sin stains and soils your good name. It brings guilt and a heavy burden. It destroys, steals and kills your will and your confidence. It causes you to go into hiding and steals your joy. It robs you of your dreams, your vision and your purpose. It makes you lose your focus in life. You have everything to gain if you do not allow sin to plague you. It is time to let go of sin and to enjoy a life of fulfilment in God.

Let us examine the life of the woman who is excitedly expecting the birth of her baby. She will do anything her doctor tells her to do for the proper development and delivery of the child. She will adjust her diet, her clothing, and her activities to create a healthy and safe growth and environment for the child. She will need to stop doing some things and start doing others. She is patient and bears all the discomfort of hormonal changes and all the various adjustments that she has to make. She is so careful during this period...until the baby is born.

From then on, the baby goes through different stages of being handled, until he or she is much older and becomes independent. Liken this baby to your dream or vision – from when it was conceived until it has been realized. In similar fashion, you must be careful not to allow sin to abort it or kill it. Be mindful of the places you visit and the types of people you hang around, for the wrong places and people can contaminate you and cause you to miscarry your dreams.

Do not say that you can take care of yourself when you hang out with the wrong people. It probably will not be long before you will join them and defile yourself with sin. So if you still have friends that have a negative hold on you, redefine your relationships and make a firm decision to cut yourself away from them so you can fulfil your destiny without any waste of time. In times past, I have had to cut myself off from friends who made a mockery of my new life in Christ. Each time we were together, they wanted to make me live as my former self in a sinful life. I had to cut off those close ties but without any anger or animosity. I took away from them the power to pull me back into sin. At first, it was not easy, because they were my confidants. But with time, I began to make new Christian friends. 1 Corinthians 15:33 says:

> *"Be not deceived, evil communications corrupt good manners.*

Michal, king David's wife, became barren and remained that way until she died because she despised David in her heart when he danced before the Lord. To despise people and the things of God can stop you from being fruitful (II Samuel 6-16).

There was an occasion in my life many years ago, when I resented a brother in the church because he was living in sin. Most people knew about it and yet he kept on working in the church and was very busy with the work of God. I did not like listening to whatever he had to say. One day the Holy Spirit rebuked me and said that the brother was His son and that he loves to do God's work. He said that I should pray for him to repent. Suddenly a special love towards him flooded into my heart. I repented and began to pray for him. Not too long afterwards, he repented of that sin and everyone also knew that he was now a changed man. He kept on working for the Lord consistently. Please do not resent anyone, but pray that all may come to repentance.

Do your best to live right before God by the power of the Holy Spirit who lives in you and you will surely fulfil your goal in life

CHAPTER 14 - Spiritual Parasite
A key to laziness

It is not wise to be too dependent on people, like your friends, family, or your pastors. Being dependent oftentimes leads to laziness, which is a key obstacle to doing exploits for God. It is good to be there for one another and lend help and support to each other at times, but it becomes dangerous when you are over dependent on people and can no longer reason and think for yourself. It is no good if you are always waiting for others to make decisions for you and tell you what to do, as this makes it easy for you to become a spiritual parasite.

A spiritual parasite always expects their pastor or other people to pray for them, and they do not pray for themselves -- *or* for others. What they do not realize is that they are in better position to pray for themselves, because they know more about their own situation than others. Other people can – and *should* – only pray along, in agreement with them. A spiritual parasite is not creative or imaginative. It is easier for them to ask people for solutions, even for the smallest of things. They shut out themselves from reasoning and over esteem others above themselves. They don't work on their self-confidence, so they achieve nothing for themselves because of themselves.

In the Bible, David thought for himself. He knew within himself that he could kill Goliath, even when those around him thought he was like them and could *not* do it. You are not like every other person. You are unique and have all it takes to be successful. God planned it that way, especially for every Believer. Even the beautiful butterfly has always been on the inside of the caterpillar, but only when it was time, would it go into the cocoon where metamorphosis takes place. No butterfly before its time. Before its transformation, the caterpillar looks awful and it crawls. After becoming a butterfly, it becomes beautiful, and grows wings and flies. So, dig into those creative abilities that God has deposited inside of you before you were born. Use your power of imagination and creativity, and the Word of God to create your miracle. Don't slow down yourself by being too dependent on people. You will be surprised at what you find and what you are able to do through Christ.

People can speak the mind of God over your life some of the time, but not all of the time, and it's because, they know in part, and can speak to your life, or *into* your life, in part. But only you can know more about the will of God concerning your life. So break away from being dependent on people, for only then can you really think clearly and dig deep into yourself and discover what God has deposited in you.

Hebrews 5:12 – 14 says:

> *"And you have come to need milk and not solid food. For everyone who partakes only of milk is unskilled in the word of righteousness for he is a babe. But solid food belongs to those who by reason of use have their senses exercised to discern both good and evil."*

So examine yourself to know whether you have attained full age to stand on your own faith. And if not, change – grow up, because stunted growth will hinder you achieving your goal. It is scriptural to share with one another and depend on each other's faith, but make sure that you do not give the place of God in your life to your pastor, your family, or your friends. Do not over-depend on others for anything in life. It is like selling your birthright to someone else to fashion your life. You are in effect licensing someone to control you.

There are times when you are in a difficult situation and you are trying to make people understand what you are going through. It can be very difficult for them to know what you are experiencing, so they may begin to counsel you without a proper understanding of what you are trying to communicate. You alone know the reality of what you are experiencing. And you are the best person to present the matter before the presence of God.

To you who are a confidant to someone who is leaning on you, my advice is to help the over-dependent person to stand on his or her own two feet or, in essence, to stand on their own faith. Do so in love; do not do their thinking for them.

True love will make you want to help someone to be independent. It will make you deny yourself of the enjoyment and satisfaction you derive out of controlling someone else's life. Once the person knows you are going to ask them to solve their problems without your opinion, they will gradually break away from coming to you for solutions. They will begin to pray more for themselves, and believe more for themselves. They will think more for themselves and do more for themselves. And it is important for every Christian to dig deeper into themselves to bring out the deposit of success that God placed on the inside of them.

Some years ago, I went to meet with my pastor for prayer over a matter. He rebuked me sharply and told me to go and pray over it myself. He said that I ought not to have come to him over such matters but should go to God myself. I felt all alone with God and went to the altar of the church. I knelt down and prayed and cried my heart out before the Lord, and He answered me in due time. This was a very good rebuke for me, because this incident helped me to not run after prayer from anyone. I began to pray more for myself, and every now and then I could also ask people to come in agreement with me over a matter, but I prayed more and believed more for myself.

So many people underestimate themselves and don't believe in themselves, so they rely on others in all that they do. But if you are that way, it is time to wake up to reality. Quit being lazy. Put your trust in God and learn to be dependent on Him, by making Him your everything. The truth is that creativity comes when a person is in touch with his true identity and looks inward to the kind of person he or she really is. This can be achieved only when a person thinks for himself. Jesus, our perfect example, asked the people questions that made them think and caused them to respond for themselves. When they wanted a miracle, He would say, *"Do you believe that I am able to do this?"* (Matthew 9:28) or if they wanted healing, He might say, *"Do you want to get well?"* (John 5:6), or *"Who do you think I am?"* (Mark 8:17).

CHAPTER 15 - Spiritual Maturity
The basis of working with God at all times

Do all you can to mature spiritually. You don't want to go around in circles in life, without visible growth or change. There are a lot of things to accomplish in life, and that is why we must not remain stagnant but advance in life. Do not be satisfied with just being saved and preparing for the rapture. You are still alive, so work for God, because He has a lot of things for us to do before joining Him in glory.

In Philippians 1:21, Paul says:

> *"For to me to live is Christ, and to die is gain."*

As long as you live, as Christ, be determined to work tirelessly for God. And, be creative like Him. Be a blessing to your world, and touch the lives that come in contact with yours. Let your life be an encouragement to others.

Also John 9:4 says:

"I must work the works of Him who sent me while it is day, the night cometh when no man can work."

There are many services to be rendered in your local church. Join a group and serve diligently. As you do, the Lord will begin to gradually lead you into greater and greater things. The work of God is not for a certain few in the church. It is for everyone and there is room for all to faithfully serve. We cannot all be preachers, but we can clean the church. We can be stewards, evangelists, singers or musicians. We can be Sunday School teachers or serve in many other areas. The more work we do for God, the more of vacuum we discover we have inside us. We find more the need to be refilled over and over again, and this process causes us to grow and mature in knowledge in many different areas of our lives.

As we know, stagnant water has an awful odor. It collects dirt and is not fresh and therefore is not healthy for consumption. So it is when your life is stagnant and not being really resourceful. You cannot help yourself, let alone someone else. Learn to make yourself useful. When you are jobless, do volunteer work in the interim. Keep yourself busy, for if you don't, the devil will fill your mind with evil thoughts, words and deeds.

But as you keep yourself busy and continue in prayer and reading the Word, this will continue to renew, and refresh you. you then will become like flowing waters that restore the soul with fresh, creative ideas springing up from your inner man.

It is a great joy for parents to watch their children grow from total dependence on them to being able to feed and care for themselves. And, of course, finally the children become financially independent and start their own families. This is healthy for man, as it gladdens the heart as we do what pleases God – become fruitful and multiply.

I encourage you to stop doing same old things without advancing in life. Put your trust in God and be prepared to take risks. Dare to do things by yourself and stop being dependent on others.

CHAPTER 16 - My Personal Encounter with the Holy Spirit

The giver of power and momentum to create

I received Jesus into my life in 1985. After that, I desired to be baptized in the Holy Spirit with the evidence of speaking in tongues. But nothing happened. I was always responding to altar calls to be prayed for by different preachers. I saw many people who were baptized in the Holy Ghost but , when I would not receive, I got so disturbed. Finally, I made up my mind to go to God myself. So I locked myself in the room and began to praise and worship God. All of a sudden, the Holy Ghost power came mightily upon me and I began to sing in tongues. From then on, each time I would pray, I could not control myself. I prayed so loudly that it seemed everywhere was quaking. I told one of my pastors, and he counseled me with the Word of God, saying that I could control this power within me. And over time, it was so, and I was able to control myself. After then, I began to discover various gifts in my life as I was faithfully serving in my local church.

The Holy Spirit gives us special strength, a special anointing and the momentum to do whatever we need to do at any given time. So desire to be baptized in the Holy Ghost if you have not received that gift already. If you have, be wise enough not to channel that energy down a wrong course. Use the gifts of the Spirit wisely.

After nineteen years of working on this book, I knew when it was time to publish it because I had this special drive in me to complete it. So, I had to carve out time and resist the temptation to do something else. I made a lot of sacrifices to make it a reality.

In the story of Creation that is recorded in Genesis, God did everything in order. He did not make man before light, or water, or lands, or animals, but He *did* make man before woman. So we ought to be doing certain things at every given stage of our lives. It becomes very frustrating and time-wasting when enthusiasm meant for one thing is misdirected toward something else – another goal, for instance. God may have given you a business idea which you were once very excited about, but because you did nothing to attain that goal, you allowed yourself to be distracted by something else.

Some years ago in Nigeria, we had an all-night prayer in the church, but I could not attend because I had to work late and was tired. I prayed that God would send an angel with my blessing to my house. So, that night, in my dream, an angel came to me in a female form. She had wings and she told me that I was blessed. She taught me this song, and we both sang and praised God until I woke up. The song goes like this:

> "Jesus you are worthy,
> You are worthy, you are worthy
> You are worthy to be praised"

When I woke up, an anointing was on me so great that I felt my head was going to burst. I began to pray, but it increased the more. The Holy Spirit then told me that I needed to go and evangelize an area in the community where I lived. It took me about three days to figure out precisely what God wanted me to do. Finally, I went to witness in that particular area with great urgency and passion, and I was filled with great power and strength. After a few weeks of preaching there, I began to settle in that anointing and power and I gradually became light headed. I later understood that without that special anointing and power, it would have been very difficult for me to preach the gospel in that area, because the hearts of the people were closed to the Gospel. But I preached without being discouraged because I knew that

God, Who sent me out there, was doing something in the hearts and lives of those people.

The special anointing that came upon me was to evangelize in that specific area at that specific time. But can you imagine what the outcome would have been if I had got it all wrong – if I had done something else or had gone somewhere else and did my own thing? As a matter of fact, you need the Holy Spirit to guide you and to teach you all things. Only the Holy Spirit can give you clarity of mind in order for you to achieve your purpose here on earth.

John 14:26 says:

> *"But the comforter, which is the Holy Ghost, whom the father will send in my name, He shall teach you all things, and bring to your remembrance, whatsoever I have said unto you"*

Re-examine your interests and your goals to be sure that they are aligned with the will of God. In order not to have a life of struggles, you need the infilling of the Holy Spirit with the manifestation of the fruits in you, namely love, joy, peace, longsuffering, gentleness, goodness, faith, meekness and temperance. Having these fruits in you provides you with the wherewithal to exceed, and there will be no limit to what God can create in and through you. Having fellowship with the Holy Spirit on a daily basis is very sweet. It is also very powerful, because you get to know the Lord better.

I love Him so much that we have this amazing relationship. He tickles me and makes me laugh, and sometimes we dance and play together. I like blowing kisses to Him. We really do have fun together most of the time. He speaks to my heart and rebukes me when I do wrong, and I have had instances in time past when the Holy Spirit would jolt me to wake me out of a deep sleep to pray. I speak to Him about almost everything that I do. Sometimes, I miss Him if I have been too busy to enjoy Him. Then I apologize to Him and straightaway He causes me to laugh. Even as I was writing this sentence, He caused me to laugh, saying "Here we go now." I laughed, and laughed, and laughed. I thoroughly enjoy my relationship with my Lord. Never trade the fellowship of the Holy Spirit for anyone or anything else. Learn to enjoy spending time with Him.

I really love God very much. Practically everything I have done throughout my life has been because I was persuaded that it was God's will for me. Sometimes I made mistakes and repented, and I tried to listen to Him again more attentively so that I could do what was right. It gives me great joy knowing that I am ready to talk about Him to the world and declare that I am not ashamed to do whatever He wants me to do in this end time. I hope and pray that you will desire Him as I do. Do all it takes to have the same or an even greater relationship and fellowship with the Holy Spirit.

Some years ago, the Holy Spirit told me to be a teacher for Adult Sunday School, but I gave Him every excuse why I could not teach. For some reason, I never liked the teaching profession, let alone becoming a Bible teacher in the church. Practically every Saturday at 4:00 p.m., there was a preparatory class for teachers to attend before they would be allowed to teach on Sundays. I thought that I was very clever. I deliberately preoccupied myself with other things at that time. After a few months of refusing to teach, the Holy Spirit left me and I became empty and ignored the scripture in Ephesians 4:30:

> *"And grieve not the Holy Spirit of God, whereby ye are sealed unto the day of redemption."*

It was a very bad experience for me because, I went through torture as my body became very heavy. Every step I took was like taking ten! It was even difficult for me to lift my arms or hands to eat! No one knew what I was going through except me. I was still going to work and to church, and was keeping up with my daily chores, albeit with great difficulty. I was miserable and could not continue in that state anymore. I cried and repented before God, Who is always faithful and forgiving. I made a promise that if the Holy Spirit should come into my life again, I would become the Bible teacher that He wanted me to be. So I waited and kept checking within me to know if He had come. The exciting news is that, after three weeks of repentance, He came to me with His sweetness, and I thanked Him. I was so happy.

Well, the very next Saturday, I attended the Sunday School preparatory class. The rules of becoming a teacher stipulated that a person must have attended three classes before they would be allowed to teach on Sunday. But there I was with the leader of the group telling me that I was going to teach the next day because there were not enough teachers available that Sunday. So I pleaded with him, telling him that I did not have enough experience to teach yet. I said that he should let me learn more, but he refused. I felt that I was going to melt, but I finally agreed to do it

The next day, that very special Sunday came when I was to teach the class. There I was, reading my manual like a newscaster because I could not really summarize the material. Immediately when the class was over, I felt like running away. I felt bad and thought that I had made a serious blunder. But I knew I had to teach again, as I did not want the Holy Spirit to leave me. Well, I got better each time I taught and later actually began to enjoy it. I remained a teacher until 2002, when I relocated to Europe. God is so faithful. He doesn't always call the qualified, but He qualifies the called.

I was blessed and was also a blessing to many through the teaching of the Word of God. I gained a lot of knowledge and experience as I attended various teaching conferences, all of which made me who I am today. I thank the Lord God Almighty for such a great learning experience in the process that I went through to prepare me for today's victory.

You may be refusing to do what God wants you to do right now for some reason. I encourage you to repent and obey Him, even if you do not understand why you are doing it. It is always for your good, as God is leading you to your destiny. Choose to trust Him with your whole life. He will never let you down. He will never put you to shame.

CHAPTER 17 –
The Alphabetic Letters of Triumph

A – Above all, adore Jesus

B – Be bold to break and destroy the works of the wicked

C – Create miracles from within you

D – Dare to be yourself and dare to take a step of faith to do something towards your goal

E – Exalt God and excel in all your ways

F – Face God in the face of fear

G – Grow great in grace, glory and wisdom

H – Have faith in God for deliverance

I – In all things, in everything, inquire of the Lord

J – Jesus is the lover of my soul

K – Keep your heart and feet from evil

L – Let go of whatever stops you from moving forward

M – Move mountains out of your way by faith in the Word of God

N – Never, never, never give up on your dreams

O – Obedience opens doors of opportunity to greatness

P – Pray until you get your breakthrough

Q – Quench not the Holy Spirit of God in you

R – Rest in God's love, peace and prosperity

S – Sing songs of praise unto the Lord

T – Testify about the goodness of the Lord

U – Update, uplift and uphold yourself with the Word of God

V – Victory is yours through the blood of Jesus Christ

W – What a mighty good God we serve

X – Excellent is God's name and excellent is His power

Y – You are blessed every day, in your going out and your coming in

Z – Zoom off with zeal to change your world with the power of God in you

SELF-EXAMINATION

1. When was the last time you prayed *for* yourself and studied the bible *by* yourself?

2. When was the last time you fasted and prayed specifically concerning your situation?

3. When was the last time you prayed for your church, pastors, and loved ones?

4. When was the last time you heard from God personally?

5. When was the last time you made decisions on your own by standing on the Word of God?

6. When was the last time you went to church with excitement?

7. When was the last time you went to church without being followed up by someone?

8. When was the last time you obeyed God without giving Him excuses?

9. When was the last time you took a bold step of faith to do a new thing?

10. When was the last time you paused and thought about your situation without telling others about it first?

LOVE CREED

I love Jesus, because He first loved me

I love my neighbor as myself

I love all the wonder of God's love

I love all the wonders of Creation

I love the times we are in, because I am equipped and ready for them

I love to change the world with God's love

I love to be a blessing to my generation

I love to lift up the name of Jesus above every other name

I love to bless the name of the Lord most high

I love to do the work of God with passion

I love to preach the Word of God and set the captives free

I love to evangelize the nations for Jesus

I love to walk in love because love is a very powerful tool that conquers all things

PRAYER:

Dear Lord, help me to discover the purpose why I was born. I pray that I will not live here on earth without achieving that goal. I pray also that I will not die with my dreams, but I will fulfil them by the power of the Holy Ghost, in the name of Jesus Christ. Amen!

Lightning Source UK Ltd.
Milton Keynes UK
UKOW021033111111

181897UK00001B/1/P